Last Summer
of the
Century

EVENING POST

in association with
JESSOPS

Last Summer
of the
Century

Edited by
David Harrison

Published by

Broadcast
BOOKS

Broadcast Books
4 Cotham Vale
Bristol BS6 6HR

Cover Photographs:

Front: (clockwise fron top left) Mary Southcott playing her violin outside the Lord Mayor's Chapel, Park St.
The Actor John Hurley with playwright Bob Fannini on the waterfront
Oliver Stokes posting a letter for his mum
Stanley Robbins enjoying a chef's break in the Wills Hall, University of Bristol. The students had all left on June 19th
Drinks at lunchtime for Bristol office workers outside the Waterfront Pub at Jury's Hotel
John the barber at Dolphin market, giving Edwin Smith a trim
An afternoon canter along a Saltford bridleway

Back: Paula the lollipop lady outside St. Mary Redcliffe School, at 3.30 pm
A limited edition millennium bench at Cadbury Garden Centre
Relaxing on College Green outside Bristol Cathedral
Sandra Demer selling the Evening Post in the corner shop in Kingsdown
Darren Clark and Alma Blackmore from the 269 Venture Scouts Unit, helping to fight drug dealers in Knowle West

Contents

Acknowledgments

This book would not have been possible without the generosity of Jessops Photo Centres, who donated cameras to Evening Post readers for this project, and developed the prints.

The pictures in this book were taken by the people of Bristol and by the Evening Post Photographic team. The final picture selection was made by Rob Stokes, David Harrison, Catherine Mason, Lu Hersey and Drew Marland.

We would like to give special thanks to Michelle Smith for her help with the pre-production scanning, and vital assistance was also given by Peter Watson, Paul Bagust, Kelvin Isles, Roger Jonathan and Hugh Dixon.

Cover and book design by Sava Fratantonio.

Printed by Bath Press, Lower Bristol Rd, Bath.

Introduction
by David Harrison

The afternoon sun breaking through
the clouds to light the ancient
standing stones at Stanton Drew

The First Millennium

People have lived in what is now the Bristol area for almost as long as there have been people. There are prehistoric remains on Redland Green and at Druid Stoke; barrows, hill forts and earthworks across south Gloucestershire and north Somerset, and the remains of a huge temple at Stanton Drew.

Bristol itself grew slowly out of the natural shape of the landscape.

The Avon was probably an important river highway (and potential invasion route) and there were armed camps on the Downs and in Leigh Woods. They controlled the ford which enabled the river to be crossed at low tide, just below where Brunel later built his Suspension Bridge. That crossing remained until 1894 when it was blown up as a hazard to shipping.

Important tracks ran through the area, and the high point of the Downs gave clear views as far as South Wales, the hills above Bath and the Mendips.

There was probably a port here and perhaps the great bluestones of Stonehenge were rafted up the Avon on their long journey from West Wales.

Then the Romans moved in.

Bristol was never a Roman town like Bath or Cirencester, but the Romans probably took over the strategic British camps and there were a number of country villas built for gentlemen farmers at Brislington, Novers Hill, and Lawrence Weston among other places.

There was also an important port where the river Trym meets the Avon at Sea Mills. The Romans needed a secure river crossing from England to the legionary fortress of Caerleon (Isca Silurum) and Sea Mills (Abona) was a sheltered harbour.

Abona was built in the 1st century AD and probably lasted until the end of the Roman occupation some three centuries later. At this point, the Bristol area largely disappears from recorded history for 600 years. It seems probable that two small settlements grew up on either side of the important Bristol bridge. On one side was Bristol which was in the kingdom of Mercia and the diocese of Worcester: on the other, Redcliffe, which was in Wessex and the diocese of Wells. That was around the fifth century, but it wasn't long before the West Saxons pushed north, and Bristol and much of Gloucestershire became part of the kingdom.

Even so the Bristol-Redcliffe division survived, leading to bitter rivalry and even armed battles until 1373 when Bristol became a city and county and swallowed up Redcliffe. Little is known of this time, although there are documents about religious houses founded at Westbury-on- Trym and Henbury as far back as the 7th century. There are stories about Alfred, the Saxon leader and first great English king hiding in Redcliffe caves after being defeated by the Danes. Perhaps he did, but his real fame was won further south in the Wessex heartlands of Somerset. Alfred's grandson Athelstan completed the overthrow of the Danes in 927 and the kings of Wessex became the kings of England for the next century and a half.

Some Saxon-style churches survive locally - Werburgha, commemorated in St Werburghs, was a Saxon saint - although which, if any, were built before the Norman invasion isn't clear. And there is what appears to be a Saxon stone coffin lid on show in Bristol Cathedral.

Apart from that (and legends about Bristol being founded by Trojan war veterans Brennus and Belinus), only one tiny remnant of history offers any clue to Bristol's place in Saxon society.

A coin from the realm of Ethelred II (978-1016) which in a Stockholm museum was minted in Bristol (Brig or Bric stow, the place of the bridge).

So the settlement was important enough to have a mint before the Norman conquest which suggests it was a trading centre by an important river crossing and a base for merchants travelling by sea to Wales and Ireland. Then the Normans came and everything changed.

12th Century

If it hadn't been for the townsfolk of Bristol, the whole course of English history might have been very different. It was all to do with Bristol's importance as the main Saxon port for Ireland, and its links with the last Saxon king, Harold.

The quarrelsome Godwin family - Earl Godwin of Wessex and his sons Sweyn, Harold, and Leofwine - were finally outlawed in 1051 by Edward the Confessor.

Sweyn had seen which way the wind was blowing and had a ship ready in Bristol, but it was Harold and Leofwine who used it to flee to Dublin where they were warmly welcomed by the Vikings who ruled much of eastern Ireland.

Twelve years later, fortunes had changed and Harold Godwinson was Earl of Wessex. In 1064, he sailed from Bristol on an expedition against the Welsh.

Harold later became king by subterfuge, insisting Edward the Confessor had named him as his successor despite outraged claims to the contrary by Duke William of Normandy.

Harold defeated his renegade brother, Tostig, and the king of Norway at Stamford Bridge, then force marched to Hastings to meet William. There the last Earl of Wessex was killed and his exhausted army slaughtered.

Bristol seems to have accepted the invaders without incident, but Exeter, where Harold's family had fled, held out until 1068. His sons escaped, possibly via Steep Holm, to the Dublin Vikings who had befriended their father and made plans to reconquer England with Irish help. Their fleet sailed up the Avon, looting villages as it came and attacked Bristol. No one knows what fortifications Bristol had then, but the invaders were driven off and that threat to the Norman conquest fizzled out.

But it wasn't surprising that the Irish Vikings aided Harold's sons - Saxon Bristol was an important trading partner, sending slaves (often passing strangers) as slaves to Ireland until Bishop Wulfstan of Worcester campaigned successfully against the practice.

And it may have been the realisation that Bristol was the key to the whole Severn Valley that led to the building of Bristol Castle.

The first Bristol castle was built by Geoffrey de Coutances, a warrior bishop who had fought at Hastings and who had big West Country estates. It was little more than a simple earth hill with a tower on top, surrounded by a ditch and enclosed land. But Geoffrey and his kinsman Roger de Mowbray later used it as a base for an unsuccessful uprising against William Rufus, the Conqueror's successor, and the king made sure from then on that such a vital fortress was in the hands of a loyal baron.

Around 1121, Robert Fitzroy, one of Henry I's illegitimate sons, was made Earl of Gloucester, and it was he who built the stupendous stone castle which dominated the city until Cromwell had it demolished.

Robert also founded the Priory of St James where he was eventually buried, and much of which still survives today. It was at this time that Bristow became Bristol on coins - possibly because it was simpler to say in the local accent.

The Earl was a strong supporter of Empress Matilda in the disastrous civil war with King Stephen, and the castle was their headquarters from where brutal mercenaries terrorised the countryside. in 1141, Stephen himself was captured and imprisoned there.

It was around this time that Robert Fitzharding - a childhood playmate of the future Henry II at a Bristol school - started the building of St Augustine's Abbey which later became the cathedral. Fitzharding was later created Lord of Berkeley.

This was the era when the Knights Templar set up the church in the area that bears their name, and the Earl of Gloucester's chamberlain was Lewin, son of Aelric, who gave his name to Lewin's Mead. And by the time the century ended, Bristol was an important manufacturing town with professional guilds who had been awarded special trading privileges.

13th Century

The early years of the 13th century saw Bristol getting its first mayor, imprisoning a princess for life and inventing what has been described as "persuasion by dentistry". By now the town was a vital centre in the West country, dominating the important Severn Valley and loyal to the Angevin kings of which John was the last.

John was determined to have no rivals, particularly Prince Arthur of Brittany and his sister Eleanor. So Eleanor was imprisoned in Bristol Castle until she died in 1241 to ensure she could have no children to threaten the Angevin claim to the throne.

In 1210, John needed to raise money for a war against the Irish, and Bristol Castle was the collecting point for money exacted from England's Jewish communities. Bristol had had a small colony of Jews since about 1100 and a ritual bath discovered in Jacobs Wells Road in 1986 is believed to be the oldest in Europe. John had the entire Jewish community arrested and taken to the castle where they were invited to donate the modern equivalent of £33 million to his war coffers. One Bristol Jew refused and had a tooth forcibly extracted each day for eight days until he gave in. It was this incident which was memorably described as "persuasion by dentistry" by historian Bryan Little.

The death of King John in 1216 and the hasty crowning of the young Henry III at Gloucester led to Bristol becoming a stronghold of the new Plantagenet dynasty. With the French still threatening, a council was held in Bristol Castle at which the Magna Carta was formally reissued under the guarantees of the papal legate and the Earl of Pembroke, Henry's guardian.

Henry remained in Bristol for several months and gave the town the right to choose its first mayor, Adam le Page, and sheriff. The powerful Berkeley, de la Warr, Gaunt and de Gournay families founded many of the town's hospitals and schools in this period, including St John's hospital, Redcliffe; St Catherine's hospital and a hostel for female lepers in Bedminster, a refuge for male lepers at Lawrence Hill; St Bartholomew's Hospital at the bottom of Christmas Steps, and St Marks, the church of which is now the Lord Mayor's Chapel.

There were a number of new religious houses, too, and it was monks who built the fresh water conduits from the hill springs around the town. Many of the conduits still exist today.

Bristol was now one of the greatest ports of the land, exporting wool and importing wine from Gascony but hampered by the tides of the Avon. So the harbour was extended and a new bridge was built to Redcliffe - then still an independent and powerful rival to Bristol with better deep water berths.

With the backing of the king, Bristol carried out one of the biggest engineering feats of the medieval years - the digging of St Augustine's Trench to give ocean going ships access to the centre of the town. Redcliffe was not pleased, especially when Henry ordered the town to help Bristol pay for the work. But it was a spectacular project which still survives as St Augustine's Reach and the buried waterway beneath The Centre.

When political reformer Simon de Montfort - said to be the founder of the House of Commons - rebelled against the king, Bristol backed de Montfort - a problem for Henry as the castle had been strengthened against the Welsh and was one of the strongest in the land. Bristol sent a fleet of ships to help de Montfort cross the Severn in 1265 and 11 were lost in a battle near the mouth of the Usk. De Montfort was forced to march overland and was defeated and killed at the battle of Evesham. Bristol was fined £1,000 for backing the wrong side and lost its grant for repairing the town walls.

In 1275, Bristol became a refuge for Jews fleeing the persecution of Queen Eleanor but in 1290, they, too, were expelled from England. It was 400 years before Bristol had a Jewish community again. But the town recovered from royal displeasure over the rebellion and by the end of the century had its first MP.

14th Century

This was the century of civil war in Bristol, an infamous death by red hot poker, and plague, blankets and charters.

The Berkeley family, which had done so much for the town, wasn't happy with Bristol's drift away from feudalism and towards self government through a mayor and council. The Berkeleys were still the Lords of Bedminster and Redcliffe on the Somerset side of the river and jealous of their privileges. But when Berkeley soldiers arrested a Bristol man in Redcliffe, Bristolians marched across Bristol Bridge and rescued him. It led to further disturbances and pitched battles between Bristol and Redcliffe men which only ended when Redcliffe was annexed to Bristol in 1373.

Matters got worse in 1307 when a new Royal Constable was appointed who demanded total obedience. The townsfolk responded by building a wall to cut off the castle from the town.

Edward II set up a Royal Commission but chose Lord Berkeley - hardly an impartial observer - to lead it and packed it with chosen outsiders. The result was a riot in which 20 people were killed.

Bristol was now in open rebellion against the crown and other royal officials were assaulted and imprisoned. But Edward was more concerned with a terrible famine and his disastrous defeat at Bannockburn, and didn't move against Bristol until 1316.

That summer, a royal army and fleet arrived (the ships were commanded by Lord Berkeley) and the castle began bombarding the town with artillery. In July, Bristol surrendered and was heavily fined, but most of the leading rebels were pardoned.

Edward needed all the support he could get in his growing struggle against his barons, and even helped pay for battle damage to be repaired. Bristol repayed him by executing two leading barons, including one of the de Montforts.

But the tide turned and when Edward's queen, Isabella and her lover, Roger Mortimer, openly rebelled, Bristol joined them. Edward's favourite, Hugh Despenser, was Constable of the castle and his 90 year old father was captured by the Bristol mob and hanged, drawn and beheaded.

Edward abdicated in 1327 and was imprisoned in Bristol Castle. There were rumours of a plan to rescue him so he was brutally force-marched to Berkeley Castle where he was appallingly treated before being murdered - allegedly with a hot poker to avoid leaving marks on his skin. The abbey of St Augustine in Bristol refused to give him burial (its patrons were Edward's enemies, the Berkeleys) and the body was taken to Gloucester. The incident could be said to mark the beginning of the end of Bristol as a centre of strategic importance, but it continued to grow as a great trading town.

A high quality cloth industry grew up in Temple and Redcliffe, and goods passing through the port included wine, grain, furs (including cat and squirrel), hides, fish, vegetables, salt, cheese and butter, oil, hemp and even woad.

The spectacular rebuilding of St Augustine's Abbey by Abbot Edmund Knowles was completed, despite a terrible outbreak of bubonic plague - the Black Death - in 1348 in which half the population of Bristol died.

It was around that time that a merchant called either Thomas or Edmund Blanket popularised the woollen sheet that bears his name, while in 1373, Bristol and Redcliffe were united in the new town and county of Bristol - separate for the first time from both Gloucestershire and Somerset. The new town had a population of around 10,000 - the second biggest provincial town after York.

15th Century

The 15th century for Bristol was the century of trade and exploration.

Bristol's merchant venturers travelled far and wide and there is circumstantial evidence that they got as far as Newfoundland, and possibly mainland America, years before Cabot and Columbus.

They were seeking new fishing grounds after German traders forced them out of the traditional Icelandic fisheries, and a fresh source of the valuable dye that created the much admired Bristol Red cloth. They certainly found the fish.

The next stage occurred after the Wars of the Roses in which some Bristolians fought on the Yorkist side and Edward IV visited a couple of times to remind Bristolians who was in charge.

Edward died and his brother, Richard III, is rumoured to have murdered Edward's sons in the

Tower of London. Richard himself was overthrown by Henry Tudor in 1485, at which point Bristol comes back in the story.

It was Henry (the seventh of that name) who agreed to back Italian adventurer Giovanni Caboto and his sons to join in the search for new lands across the western seas.

Caboto - better known locally as John Cabot - set out in 1497 and probably got at least as far as Newfoundland and Nova Scotia.

The journey gained Cabot a pension, the money being paid by customs official and Bristol landowner Richard Ameryk who may have been involved in the secret earlier trips to the rich Newfoundland fishing grounds. One theory even suggests America was named after Ameryk.

Cabot went back in 1498 with Henry's blessing and vanished from history. He may have been shipwrecked off Newfoundland as local tradition has it; he may have been killed by the Spanish on mainland America, he may have come home and quietly retired. No one knows.

But the dominant figure of the time was not Cabot but William Canynges, four times mayor, MP, and owner of (by medieval standards) a massive fleet of ships. He employed a sizeable percentage of the workers of Bristol - some 900 men - and helped rebuild St Mary Redcliffe Church.

In the end, he gave away his fortune, much to his daughter-in-law's disgust, and became a priest at Westbury-on-Trym. This was the time of the Chapel of the Three Kings of Cologne, a still surviving part of John Foster's 1481 almshouses at the top of Christmas Steps; and of William Wyrecestre, the Bristol surveyor who measured and recorded the streets. There was John Jay, an early adventurer who cruised across the Atlantic (but missed America) as early as 1480; Ricart the town clerk who started the compilation of annals and records of the city known as Kalendars, and Robert Sturmey, who carried pilgrims to Jerusalem.

Sturmey was nearly the cause of a small war. The Venetians and Genoese tried to operate a monopoly on sea trade and Sturmey's competition was not welcome. In 1457, the Genoese attacked him and stole his cargo. Sturmey complained to the king and Genoese citizens in England were arrested until they compensated the Bristol merchant for his losses.

16th Century

In 1509, Sebastian Cabot sailed from a Bristol ruled by the pioneering Henry VII to seek the fabled north west passage to the far East. By the time he returned, Henry was dead and his successor, the eighth Henry, had other things on his mind than costly adventuring. But it was under Henry VIII that Bristol changed dramatically. The Thorne family, merchant venturers, founded Bristol Grammar School in the old St Bartholomew's Hospital. Sadly for the school, the deal didn't included the hospital lands, which would have made it one of the richest in Britain.

Then in 1534, Henry was declared Supreme Head of the Church in England and many of the city's religious houses were dissolved. St Mark's - Gaunt's Hospital - church became the city-owned Lord Mayor's Chapel, but the great St Augustine's Abbey was closed down.

But Henry created a new diocese of Bristol, giving the city its own bishop for the first time. Unfortunately, St Augustine's church had already been half demolished, leaving the bishop to cope in a meagre T-shaped HQ with virtually no endowments to finance it. Westbury College, where Canynges had been dean, also closed and was sold to one of the many minor nobles who were busy sweeping up former church buildings and lands.

Church plates and ornaments were sent to the Bristol Mint to be melted down and little survives from before the 1550s. Unfortunately the master of the mint was Sir William Sharington of Lacock Abbey who began issuing coins of dubious content and keeping the rest of the silver for himself. He died before he could be brought to trial on what was then a capital charge.

In 1552, the Society of Merchant Venturers was founded and immediately ran into trouble for trying to set up a trade monopoly at a time when Bristol's trade with the rest of the world was depressingly low. The city played little part in Tudor adventuring although Martin Frobisher called in on his way back from Canada with some Eskimos who thrilled locals by duck hunting from a kayak in the harbour.

One exception was Richard Hakluyt, a canon at the cathedral, who campaigned strongly for colonisation rather than occasional trading trips. His accounts of voyages and explorations inspired generations of later adventurers.

Bloody Mary's reign from 1553-1558 temporarily restored Catholicism, and led to five Bristol craftsmen being burned for heresy on St Michael's Hill. Their executioner, anxious to ingratiate himself with the queen, deliberately used green wood to make their sufferings last longer.

In 1574, her successor, Elizabeth, visited Bristol and stayed in a house that was once a Carmelite friary. She also enjoyed a mock battles in the harbour and in two specially built forts and may have said nice things about St Mary Redcliffe, although this is possibly legend. She also granted the Brandon Hill washerwomen the right to dry clothes there without being hounded by the warden - an incident recalled in a stone carving in a Corn Street bank.

As the century ended, Bristol was becoming a coal mining and metal working centre (inside Bristol Castle) as well as continuing the 400 year old tradition of soap making. Tobacco imported from the new Virginia colonies was soon being grown in Gloucestershire and a new school, Queen Elizabeth's Hospital, was founded in 1586.

Four Bristol ships were sent to help supply the English ships fighting the Spanish Armada in 1588 but the Spanish war was disastrous for the Bristol area, which lost one of its main markets. It caused great deprivation.

17th Century

When Queen Elizabeth died in 1603, her successor, James I, lost no time in making peace with Spain. It was the start of a new period of prosperity for Bristol which had suffered badly from the collapse of its traditional markets.

But it was an old style voyage of exploration from Bristol which started the new century, as Martin Pring set off for America in 1603. His expedition, which was backed by Bristol merchants John Whitson and Robert Aldworth, was to collect sassafras, a valuable medicinal herb, and to see if various European plants would grow as a prelude to a proper colony.

Pring stayed for two months and named local features Whitson Bay and Mount Aldworth in honour of his patrons. He returned in 1606 with an expedition sponsored by Sir Fernandino Gorges, Lord of Wraxall, and a number of colonies were set up in the wake of his explorations. He himself went on to help build the foundations of England's trade with India, work which gained him the nickname General to the East Indies before his death in 1627.

Bristol fisherman were, by now, openly harvesting the fertile Grand Banks off Newfoundland, and in 1610 John Guy, Sheriff of the city, took women, animals, poultry and seed to the island to set up a new permanent colony there.

It was called Bristol's Hope and it still exists as a row of modern bungalows, not far from Harbour Grace. But Guy's colony was a failure, wrecked by the fishermen's refusal to co-operate and by marauding pirates. Guy returned home in 1618 and it was left to Merchant Venturer John Barker to set up a successful colony, five years later.

At home, there were further serious outbreaks of plague between 1603-1605 and 1610-11 in which thousands died. Trade with Spain and Portugal improved and the huge St James' and St Paul's Fairs attracted traders and pirates from around the known world.

Pirates were a terrible scourge and Bristol alone lost 43 ships to them between 1609 and 1619. In 1625, Turkish raiders invaded Lundy, kidnapped Cornish villagers and threatened to burn Ilfracombe, while waiting for the heavily laden fleet from Newfoundland to arrive in Bristol.

Then, in 1625, war again flared up with Spain and two years later with the French, and a naval fleet was sent to guard Bristol merchant ships from the enemy, as well as from the assorted pirates and privateers. The wars weren't a complete disaster - the Bristol privateer Eagle took £40,000 of prizes from captured ships, and new markets were opened up with the American colonies and the Mediterranean.

As early as 1634, there was a favourite Spanish wine imported through the city called Bristol Milk, and big fortunes were being made from brass pin making.

The old Kingswood Forest, which once stretched from the Cotswolds to the Mendips, was in sad decline as deer were replaced by voracious goats, trees were chopped down to boost royal coffers, and coal mining became a major industry. Sugar refining was another money-maker, as were tobacco importing, starch-making and soap - all carried out in the face of opposition from London monopolies backed by the king.

In 1631, Captain Thomas James set out to discover the fabled north-west passage to China which Sebastian Cabot had sought in vain. He lost three men and two dogs, buried them on an island he named Brandon Hill, and wrote a book about his adventures which may have inspired Coleridge's Ancient Mariner.

In 1613, Bristol gained the second public library outside London and one Eleazer Edgar became the city's first bookseller in 1620. And in 1634, the Red Maids school for girls was founded with money from the will of merchant John Whitson.

The Civil War saw Bristol's loyalties split and Bristolians trying to ignore the whole business. The city was invaded and occupied by both sides and there is evidence that Prince Rupert intended a massacre of Parliament supporters on the first occasion he tried to take the city. A group of Royalists planned to open the Frome Gate to him but security was lax and the plotters were rounded up. Two of them, Robert Yeamans and George Boucher, were hanged, despite the personal intervention of Charles I.

Rupert finally succeeded in 1643, thanks to Colonel Henry Washington (an ancestor of the first American president) who spotted a weak point in the Parliamentary defences where Park Row now joins Park Street.

Bristol became a Royalist base, but in 1645, as the Roundhead army mopped up Royalist strongholds around the West, Rupert burned Clifton, Westbury and Bedminster and withdrew behind his new line of forts. In September he surrendered, and was allowed to march away with his men fully armed to protect themselves from the vengeance of plundered Bristolians.

After the war, Bristol was seen as a vital stronghold, especially when Welsh Royalists rebelled. And it was from Bristol that Cromwell set out to massacre Irish rebels. In 1654, he agreed to let the citizens of Bristol demolish the crumbling castle, by now a home for robbers and cutpurses.

In 1667, the city suffered another blow when Dutch raiders burned nine Bristol tobacco ships off Virginia. Bristol was making a lot of money by indenturing (virtually enslaving) the poor and the convicts as workers on the tobacco and sugar plantations. By 1670, half the city's shipping fleet was tied up in the tobacco trade, although local shipwrights also built impressive warships for Charles II.

Diarist Samuel Pepys visited in 1668, drank Bristol Milk and described Bristol as "a most large and noble place".

Nonconformists, like Baptists and the new sect of Quakers, were savagely persecuted by the bishop and others, but survived in secret. The first street was completed across the old marsh outside the city walls and named King Street in honour of the restoration, and the rich started the inexorable trek away from the stench and sickness of the city to surrounding villages like Clifton, Henbury, Brislington and Frenchay. But the century ended with more rebellion and slaughter.

In 1685, the Duke of Monmouth landed at Lyme Regis and marched north with a raggle taggle army. He got as far as Pensford and Keynsham but the Royal Army was waiting and he never reached Bristol. Ten days later, he was defeated at Sedgemoor and executed, while Judge Jeffreys brought the infamous Bloody Assizes to Bristol. He hanged some rebels, deported others and accused the mayor of Bristol of kidnapping his own citizens.

Then, in 1690, William of Orange arrived near Avonmouth, to begin his reign as William III, and was entertained at Kingsweston House. It was the beginning of a new era.

18th Century

The 18th century saw Bristol at the peak of its prosperity as a great trading city, although much of its wealth came from piracy and slavery.

City merchants were enthusiastic about privateering, under which armed merchantmen were given official backing to raid the cargo ships of other countries.

Somerset buccaneer and explorer William Dampier went hunting Spanish treasure galleons with Bristol finance, but it was the voyages of Woodes Rogers which have gained special fame.

Rogers left Bristol in 1708 with two ships to raid the Spanish in the Pacific. He burned the town of Guayaquil and captured a galleon off Acapulco, then in 1709 rescued castaway Alexander Selkirk, who had been marooned on an island for four years.

He brought Selkirk home and recorded an account of his adventure. It was read by author Daniel Defoe who may also have met Selkirk in a private home or a long vanished pub in Bristol (not the Llandoger Trow as legend has it) before using the tale as the basis for Robinson Crusoe.

There is a pair of silver candlesticks in Bristol Cathedral which was presented by Bristol's town clerk from the profits he made from investing in Rogers' voyage.

Considering that it was England's second city, Bristol played little part in national politics although it briefly had one of the new regional mints and MPs who spoke strongly on behalf of the West India traders.

This was the century of the infamous Triangular Trade. Bristol was a major import-export centre, bringing in food, raw materials, tobacco, rum, dried fruit, wine, cork and olives and exporting luxury goods, Midlands metalwork, refined sugar, coal and glass.

The West Indian and Virginian trade was vital to the city. So Bristol merchants travelled to West Africa with trade goods, exchanged them for slaves from Arab slavers or rival tribes, and took them across the Atlantic. There they were exchanged for sugar, rum and tobacco which were brought back to Bristol. It was highly profitable and by 1727, there were nearly 90 Bristol ships sailing the triangle.

Losses could be high too - many English seamen and slaves died from tropical diseases before the transatlantic voyage even began. Later, when the trade became illegal, it was not unknown for all the slaves to be thrown overboard if a warship appeared.

But Bristol also traded with the northern colonies where there were no slaves, and by 1788 there were 50 Bristol ships sailing to North America and more than 100 regularly visiting from New York and Philadelphia (founded by Bristolian William Penn) .

The city was even involved in a small way in whaling and Greenland whales were cut up and processed at Sea Mills. But even then it was obvious that the treacherous Avon was a major obstacle to sea trade (ships had to be towed along it by teams of rowing boats) and plans for a tide free harbour were put forward as early as 1767.

By now, Bristol was an important banking centre and the council hired John McAdam to make the world's first road paved in his new surfacing - tarmacadam - between Bristol and Bath.

Coal mining was a major industry in Kingswood and north Somerset, and with it came iron foundries, brassworks, zinc plating (the first in Britain), lead shot making at William Watts' revolutionary shot tower in Redcliffe, and coloured glass.

There was also the new trade of chocolate making. The first chocolate makers in the city were possibly the Churchman family who, in 1761, sold the business to Quaker Joseph Fry.

There were snuff mills, over 50 tobacconists, dozens of distilleries, more than 40 breweries, and 35 wine merchants including the company which became Harveys. Ship building and repairs were important, too, but many ordinary Bristolians still lived a life of extreme poverty and deprivation.

Queen Square - named after Queen Anne who visited in 1702 - was completed on the old Marsh, and Portland Square, Brunswick Square and the squares and terraces of Kingsdown, Clifton and Hotwells soon followed.

The rich enjoyed huge banquets of stomach churning proportions, and pleasure gardens at Lawrence Hill and on Durdham Downs. The poor had the riotous St James Fair, cockfighting, bull baiting and bloody bare knuckle boxing.

This was the era of Edward Colston, certainly a slaver but also a great benefactor to the city, and the opening of Bristol Infirmary - the first hospital funded by public subscription - in 1737.

Dr Edward Fox pioneered care for the insane while local Quakers led a strong anti-slavery movement. Bristol had the first Baptist College and saw the birth of Methodism under George Whitefield and John and Charles Wesley.

In 1772, Bristol Library Society set up up a superb library in King Street, members of which included poets Southey (later Poet Laureate), Coleridge, Wordsworth and miners' safety lamp inventor Humphrey Davey. The city was also among the first to have its own newspapers, starting with The Post Boy in 1702 and followed by numerous titles from the Farley family.

This was the time of Thomas Chatterton, forger, conman and poet, whose suicide inspired the whole Romantic movement; of "Holy Hannah" More who championed women, children and slaves; of the actress Mary Robinson who became mistress of the Prince of Wales, and Ann Yearsley, the milkmaid poet.

There had been an early attempt to build a theatre in the city which was stopped by a puritanical vicar, but a small playhouse did open at Hotwells (outside the city boundary) in the 1720s.

In 1766, Bristol finally got its first theatre, hidden discreetly behind the frontage of King Street. Twelve years later, it was given a warrant to call itself the Theatre Royal.

It was a time of rich creativity, of beautiful buildings and monuments, of glorious craftsmanship in glass, pottery and precious metals. It was also a time when the rich and famous flocked to take the waters at Hotwells and Clifton became a major resort; when Britain lost its American colonies and Bristol was seriously hurt by war with revolutionary France, and when Thomas Beddoes discovered laughing gas, tried to bleach black people, and attempted to cure TB with the wind from both ends of a cow.

19th Century

As the elegance of the Georgian era faded into the brass and iron respectability of Victoria's reign, Bristol again went up in flames. Trade had suffered badly from the latest wars against the French, and many of the grandiose (but speculative) Clifton terraces were left unfinished as money ran out. By the 1830s, the port was in serious decline, despite the completion of the New Cut and Feeder Canal in 1809 to give the city a tide-free floating harbour.

Port duties were among the highest in Britain and those, coupled with the usual problem of navigating the Avon and the drift of industry to the Midlands and north, drove away the shipping.

Slavery was about to be abolished, hitting the valuable plantation trade, and the overall standard of living was lower than many other big cities.

All this, plus the restlessness caused by the French and American revolutions and radical new ideas on freedom and democracy, led to riots across the country. Bristol's turn came in 1831 when Recorder Sir Charles Wetherell, a crusader against reform, arrived to open the Assizes. He was mobbed at Totterdown by an angry crowd and stoned as he travelled to the Guildhall.

The situation grew uglier and Wetherell fled, disguised as a servant. The mob then attacked the prisons, and burned toll houses, one side of Queen Square, the bishop's palace and the Mansion House. Many rioters, busy looting the great houses, died in the flames or beneath melting lead from the roofs. No one knows the final death toll.

Troops finally intervened and belatedly restored order, but £300,000 worth of damage had been done. Much of the stolen property was later recovered, but the riot was a terrible shock to the city. Four rioters were hanged and 77 others imprisoned or deported, but the Reform Bill was finally passed the following year.

The same year saw Clifton, St James, St Philips and St Pauls swallowed up by Bristol and abortive plans for a horse drawn tramway linking the city with the south coast. The Bristol and Gloucestershire Railway opened in 1835 to bring coal from Coalpit Heath.

It was followed by the Great Western Railway, an astonishing achievement which linked Bristol and London by 1841 and tunnelled two miles through Box Hill - an impossibility according to scientific opinion. The same year, the Bristol and Exeter Railway extended the service to Bridgwater. The railways also went to Wales although passengers had to get off at New Passage and take a ferry until the Severn Tunnel opened in 1886. Luckily, one of Brunel's ideas - a central station in Lewins Mead with a line on an embankment through Queen Square - never materialised.

In 1848, the ailing city docks were taken over by the Corporation, and numerous plans were put forward for deep water docks at the mouth of the Avon. Avonmouth opened in 1877 followed by Portishead in 1879, with railways linking them to the city.

Before that, Brunel had suggested extending his GWR line to New York via a steamship service from Bristol. He built two great ships, the Great Western in 1836-7 and the Great Britain (launched 1843) which had a long and varied career before ending up back in the city again.

Neither ship used Bristol as its English base however - both were too big and port dues were simply too high. More closely linked with the city were the Bristol Steam Navigation Company, founded in 1836, and Bristol City Line which Charles Hill formed in 1846 from an even older company owned by the shipbuilding Hillhouse company.

The West India slaves were finally freed in 1833, despite a fierce campaign by Bristol merchants. One, Thomas Daniel, received £55,000 compensation for loss of his slaves - a veritable fortune for the time.

Sugar refining took on a new lease of life with Conrad Finzel's steam process, and the ancient trade of soap making was updated at the new Christopher Thomas works in Broad Plain. Another huge new enterprise was the Great Western Cotton Works, an attempt to rival the Lancashire mills, which opened in 1838 and was initially staffed by Lancashire cotton workers. Within a few years, it employed more than 1,500 people.

Fry's Chocolate in the Pithay had 1,000 employees by the 1880s and one of its employees who in 1881 left to set up a second big chocolate company (Packers, Carsons, Famous Names and now Leaf UK) which eventually moved to Greenbank.

Tobacco was still a major force in the city and the company founded by Williams Day Wills and Henry Overton Wills in 1833 was the biggest. They began in Redcliffe, expanded to Bedminster and Ashton in 1886 and were, like Fry's, among the most enlightened employers of the time. The third of the big three was E S and A Robinson, the packaging makers, which started in a small way in 1844.

The Bristol and Somerset coalfield continued to expand with a move into deep mining. The most important mine owner was Handel Cossham, one of the first to study the geology of mining to discover where the best seams lay. He had four pits and employed 1,500 men by the time he died in 1890. But by 1887, there were 17 pits and 2,500 miners in the Bristol coalfield, and annual output was over half a million tons. Retired and disabled miners also started Kingswood's big boot and shoe industry which grew from the home cobbling trade.

Bristol became the regional stronghold of the growing trade union movement, and Bristol Trades Council was set up in 1873. In 1892, a trade union procession to collect funds for striking confectionary and dock workers was charged by police and troops and a number of strikers injured. The day was long remembered in Bristol as Black Friday.

In 1888, Bristol cathedral was finally completed, some 700 years after it was founded and in 1897, Bristol gained its own bishop again after 40 years as an outpost of the Diocese of Gloucester. Clifton became the headquarters of a new Catholic see in 1850, while Brunswick Square chapel was the scene of Britain's first legal Nonconformist wedding in 1837.

George Muller opened his first orphanage in St Pauls in 1836 before expanding to to the huge stone houses on Ashley Down where he brought up some 2,000 children. It was also the era of social reformer Mary Carpenter, pioneering doctor William Budd, and Elizabeth Blackwell, the Bristol girl who became the first woman doctor.

Bristol General Hospital was set up 1832, curiously as a working class rival to the Tory-run Bristol Infirmary, and Bristol Zoo opened in Clifton in 1835 after a plan to build it where Arno's Vale cemetery is now fell through. And Downend doctor W G Grace - grandson of eccentric George Pocock who invented a kite-drawn carriage - single handedly rewrote the history of cricket.

There was William Friese-Greene, a pioneer of cinematography, and of course, Isambard Kingdom Brunel, the outsider who stamped his mark on the city. He built the Clifton Suspension Bridge (finally opened in 1864 after his death), the main railways, the locks, water flow regulators and mud scrapers of the floating harbour, two giant ocean liners, a railway station, a luxury hotel, and various industrial buildings.

Some of the finest Victorian painters worked in Bristol, as did leading architect Edward Godwin, a friend of Oscar Wilde and lover of actress Ellen Terry, and John Percival, who turned Clifton College into a major public school.

Remarkably, Bristol still didn't have a university and a meeting was called in 1874 to set up a College of Science and Literature. It opened in two houses in Park Row in 1876 and was the first University College to admit women. But it wasn't until 1909 that it became a proper full scale university.

20th Century

The 20th century started with talk about Bristol's new tram system. It's ending with more talk about . . . Bristol's new tram system. Whether the planned new one ever gets off the ground is still under debate as the second Millennium draws to a close. But the first offered the city a public transport system which reached every suburb and was fast (for the time), clean and efficient. Horse trams had been introduced as far back as 1875 and Bristol Tramways also experimented with steam power. But as the new century opened, the city became one of the first to enjoy an electric tram system which lasted until a Second World War bomb severed power cables.

The genius behind the electric trams was Sir George White, an extraordinary man whose vision gave Bristol the biggest aircraft works in the world at Filton. He started small, with his British and Colonial Aeroplane Company making French planes under licence, but the company soon expanded into its own products like the famous Bristol Boxkite.

The Great War saw the company building the legendary Bristol Fighter (4,747 of them) then changing its name to the Bristol Aeroplane Company.

The years between the wars saw successful plane building falter, but also the development of world beating engines (Mercury, Pegasus, Hercules), as well as the RAF's standard fighter, the Bristol Bulldog. By 1935, more than 8,000 people were working at Filton and Patchway and it was there that famous Second World war planes like the Blenheim and Beaufighter were conceived.

Bristol was entrusted with developing a post war passenger plane to compete with the Americans on the transatlantic route and came up with the Brabazon, a giant offering the luxury of an ocean liner. It was the biggest plane ever built in Britain - 177 ft long with a 230 ft wing span and eight engines. But the technology was outdated by the time it flew and it never got past the prototype stage.

It was left to the Britannia (the Whispering Giant), the supersonic Concorde, collaborations on the Eurofighter and Airbus, innovative space technology and world beating Rolls Royce aero-engines to keep the Bristol aircraft industry in the public eye.

The First World War gave a great boost to Bristol's port with tonnage nearly doubling thanks to troop and munitions ships. Some of the famous Bristol Channel White Funnel paddle steamers were called up as minesweepers and four Bristol City Line cargo ships were sunk.

Douglas Motorcycles of Kingswood dominated the racing tracks in the first half of the century, but older industries like cotton, glass and coal mining all declined and finally died.

Fry's moved its chocolate factory out of the city centre to a green field site near Keynsham in the early 20s and Avonmouth began to grow into a huge industrial site. The Port of Bristol received a boost in 1908 with the opening of the Royal Edward Dock, but it was too late to recapture the trade lost to Liverpool and elsewhere.

The Depression hit Bristol in the 30s but not so badly as the Midlands and north. The key lay in the diversity of employment on offer - building, transport distribution, packaging, engineering footwear, furniture, clothing, chemicals, tobacco and paint companies all employed thousands of workers.

In 1919, Bristol started a huge programme of slum clearance and new building which by 1939 resulted in 36,000 new homes and nine new council estates on the outskirts. The city also swallowed up neighbouring villages in Gloucestershire and Somerset, but the vast (and aggressive) expansion of Bristol Tramways bus services and the growth of family motoring encouraged more people to move out of Bristol itself and into rural areas.

Bristol produced Ernest Bevin who made his name as a Bristol dockworkers' leader; Archie Leach who became a Hollywood heartthrob under the name Cary Grant; variety star Randoph Sutton who serenaded Mother Kelly's Doorstep, and Clara Butt, Eva Turner and Dennis Noble who dominated the opera and concert stages. Stafford Cripps, one of the greatest Chancellors of the Exchequer of the 20th century, was a Bristol MP, and William Slim became Field Marshall the Viscount Slim of Bishopston, a brilliant Second World War commander.

The Second World War changed everything. Much of the old centre of the city was blitzed and many historic buildings destroyed. The city was initially thought to be far enough away to be safe from the bombers, and London children were evacuated here, together with much of the BBC. Then the Germans invaded France and Bristol was suddenly within easy reach of the raiders. Nearly 1,300 people were killed and many hundreds injured in air attacks.

Avonmouth docks again became a focal point for troop and supply movements, especially from America, and the city airport at Whitchurch played a vital role through its links to neutral Portugal and Ireland. Clifton College became the HQ of the US 1st Army and both Bristol Aircraft Company and Bristol Tramways were involved in making warplanes at the most unlikely sites, including bonded warehouses and the new Electricity House on the Centre. More than 2,753 aircraft and more than 100,000 engines were built in Bristol during the war and another 3,000 Bristol Blenheims and Beaufighters were built elsewhere.

After 1945, Bristol began to rebuild. The main shopping area moved away from the Castle Street-Wine Street district to neighbouring Broadmead. Sadly, the dismal result was far removed from the original imaginative vision, although the 90s Galleries shopping mall has helped revive the area.

The combination of bomb damage, slum clearance and redevelopment altered the balance of the city, too. Many inner city residents were moved to new estates around the outskirts and old communities were scattered. Areas like St Philips were transformed beyond belief from tightly packed houses to landscaped commercial areas. The Port of Bristol was revived with the opening of Royal Portbury deep water dock opposite Avonmouth, and while it lost the valuable banana trade, it won a new role as Britain's biggest car shipping terminal.

The huge St Anne's Board Mills closed in 1980 and tobacco processing declined as Imperial

Tobacco abandoned Bedminster for Hartcliffe and finally moved cigarette production to Nottingham. Packaging giant E S and A Robinson also went through name changes and restructuring before becoming a shadow of the company that revolutionised every day necessities like paper bags, boxes and sticky tape.

Douglas at Kingswood had a brief revival selling Italian Vespa scooters under licence but it was a short term venture. And although new breweries were set up in the city, Courages pulled out of brewing in the city in 1999.

The Colston Hall was destroyed by fire (for the second time) in the late 40s, but rebuilt and reopened in 1951, and the Theatre Royal became home to the new Bristol Old Vic Theatre Company in 1946 after decades as a rough music hall. The theatre complex was expanded in the 60s to take in the neighbouring Cooper's Hall and provide a new studio theatre, but the popular Little Theatre ended its life ignominiously as a bar for the Colston Hall. Bristol hosted the start of a post war eating revolution when the Berni brothers opened their first steak restaurant and brought dining out to ordinary people.

But by the end of the century, traditional manufacturing had virtually disappeared from the centre of the city, to be replaced by the new industries of finance, insurance, restaurants and bars, computer-related businesses and the heritage ventures like the revival of blue glass making

The city also became a nationally known centre of youth culture with a vibrant club scene and international stars like jazzman Andy Sheppard and pop idols Massive Attack, Tricky, Portishead and Roni Size. It was also noted internationally for the BBC Natural History Unit and the Wildscreen film festival. The Canons Marsh area was finally being redeveloped after half a century of indecision although Bristol's dream of an international concert hall there had evaporated.

The old Temple Meads covered goods yard - the largest in the world - had disappeared to make way for another office and hotel development, and Bristol had regained its independence after being swallowed up by the short lived county of Avon after exactly 600 years as a city and county.

Yet much of the new development was outside the actual city in neighbouring areas with motorway links - Cribbs Causeway which grew rapidly into the biggest shopping centre in the region; Emerson's Green, and the Bradley Stoke district where Europe's biggest new town and yet more offices and stores filled former farmland.

But the south side of the city was still depressed and starved of investment and there were still pockets of real poverty and deprivation in a generally prosperous city.

It is that city which is pictured in this book.

Editor's Note

We received a tremendous response to our Millennium photography competition from the people of Bristol. Our warmest thanks to all who took part. The photographs in the following pages represent only a selection of the many excellent photographs that were received; sadly, we were unable to include every photograph that we would have liked, but their omission is no reflection on their quality.

We have made every effort to find out the circumstances behind each photograph and to include personal names wherever possible. We apologise in advance for any inadvertent errors. Where there are few details it is usually because it proved impossible to trace the subjects after the photographs were taken: children playing in a distant street, people in phone boxes, etc. A few contributors also omitted to supply their names, addresses or telephone numbers. Although we have made selections from their contributions, we have been unable to trace them to thank them in person.

1.
Daybreak

The sun dawns over Bristol
on 21st June, 1999

1. Dawn over the Floating Harbour looking towards the terraces of Redcliffe, and the spire of St. Mary Redcliffe beyond

2

2.   Ewen Mcleod on Brandon Hill looking over the city at 5.10am

3

4

3.   Wapping Wharf and Prince's Wharf at 4.15 am
4.   A Weetabix breakfast for Victoria Smith

5. A morning milk order noted by Horfield milkman Dave Hughes
6. Kirsty Ford's mum Caroline waking up to breakfast at 7.15, in Leaholme Gardens, Whitchurch

7

8

7. Jennifer Smith loading the dishwasher after breakfast
8. The 19th Century Fairbairn steam crane at Wapping Wharf, built by Stothert and Pitt

2.
At Home

Clare and Jade outside
no. 1, Dingle Views,
Sea Mills

9. Becky Moss enjoying her breakfast at Alexandra Rd, Uplands
10. Gladys Donovan making a pot of tea at home in Knowle Park
11. Doreen Mallett busy at her sewing machine in Bishopsworth
12. Jenny Coles doing the dishes at home in Winterbourne

13. Doris Brooks crocheting at Hollybrook Elderly Peoples' Home, Hartcliffe
14. Mrs Clark has a well-earned drink after completing the housework
15. Emma Osborne knitting while watching the television in Broomhill Rd

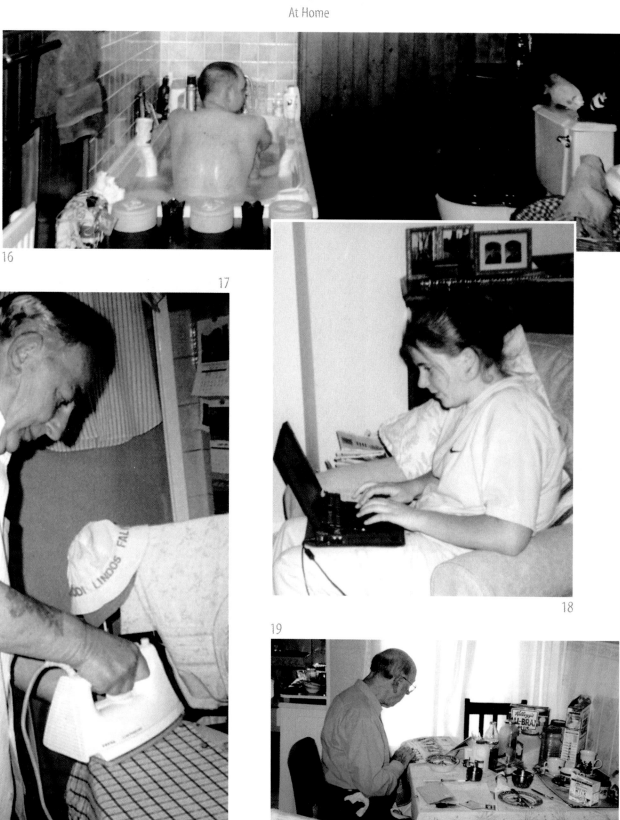

16

17

18

19

16. Anthony Bryant in the bath at home in Hambrook
17. Mr Humphries doing his share of the ironing in Merrimans Rd, Shirehampton
18. Elizabeth Ongley, age 15, using a lap-top computer
19. Tony Walsh reading his paper at breakfast

20. Gilly Nickolls tucking into strawberries and cream with her friends Diane and Brent Wilson
21. Gregory Dymond washing the floor at Nightingale House, a Care Home for people with learning difficulties
22. Nick Oswin relaxing with a book at the end of the day
23. Royston Clark tackling the cleaning in Greendale Rd

24. Sheila White kitting at home in her sitting room in Knowle
25. Clem Brown having a morning shave in Broadfield Ave, Kingswood
26. Julie Morris snapped at bedtime in Stackpool Rd, Southville
27. Darren Price hanging out the washing

3.
In the Garden

Mr Bones working on his allotment
in Cranbrook Rd

28. Mr Johnson watering his new potato plants on his Woodstock allotment
29. Jean Oswin grooving around a pole in her garden watched by husband Gordon
30. Patrick Perry's home grown produce near Oldland Common
31. John Miskin mowing around the sculpture *Refugee* by Naomi Blake (1980) in Bristol Cathedral garden

32

33

34

32. 'Where's the door?' John Thomas and Dan Maggs building a pigeon shed in Saltmarsh Drive, Lawrence Weston

33. Outside school hours, Louise is a regular volunteer at Lawrence Weston Community Farm

34. Mrs Knight in front of her delphiniums

35. Pat Thomas washing her feet in the bird bath
36. Lester Rhoomes gardening in Gordon Ave, Whitehall
37. Pat Walsh digging hard in her Logan Rd garden
38. Edwin Smith picking sweet peas in his garden at the end of the day

4.
The Working Day

Mary Southcott playng her violin outside the Lord Mayor's Chapel at the bottom of Park Street

40

39

43

44

41

42

39. Alana Lydon holding up her Rovers shirt in the kitchens at the University of Bristol

40. Cleaning for the council in Spring Hill, Kingswood

41. Richard Baker fixing a car at Five Stokes Autos, Stoke Gifford

42. Kate Maddon in the dentist's chair at Mr Pritchard's surgery, Westbury on Trym

43. Andrew Stocker, customer liason officer at the Bristol Old Vic, busy on the phone

44. Betty Sargent holding her sculpture at the Greenway Development Centre Trust, Southmead

46

49

45

47

48

45

45. Michael Bridgeman up a ladder in Court Rd

46. Kelly Moss, an assistant at Bakers Dolphin, travel agents, in their Redfield branch

47. Stanley Robbins preparing supper for the wardens of the Department of Politics at the University of Bristol

48. Francesca Senior adjusting the model of John Cabot at the Maritime Heritage Centre

49. Geoff Rawland, a stall holder in East Street, with a customer

50

51

52

53

50. Andy Wedmore at the Timpson's key-cutting booth in Whiteladies Shopping Centre

51. Phyllis mopping the floor at Badminton School - the last job of the day

52. The workshop at the new Explore@Bristol site where some of the exhibits are being created

53. Louise and Carolyn, stylists at Reflections, Nailsea

54

56

57

55

47

54. Mrs Malcahy moving house with the help of Keith
Donovan's company, KP Transport

55. BT engineer Simon Parfitt with his daughter Hayley who
is on work experience, checking lines in Whitchurch

56. John Watts on the phone at J&D Tyres

57. Perrine Wyplosz on site at the ground floor of
Explore@Bristol. To the left is the planned underground car
park

58

59

60

58. Workers at the Creda factory in Yate, making washing machines. Kathy King (back to the photographer) is talking to Sylvia Smith, while Pauline Evans and Mrs Overton are sealing the drum of the tumble dryer, and Mr Streete is checking machines in the right foreground

59. Art and Craft exhibition at St Mary's-on-the-Quay by Bristol Castle Federation of the Townswomens' Guild to celebrate 70 years of the Guild.

60. Sgt Andrew Bishop and groom Amanda West clean kit in the tack room at Bower Ashton Police Stables after the summer solstice operation at Stonehenge

61

62

63

65

64

61. Home helps Mrs Reynolds and Mrs Knight working at Latchmoor House, flats for retired people

62. Bob the postman in Whiteway Road, St George

63. A police constable making enquiries at Glen's Flower Shop in the High Street, Kingswood

64. Roger Bennett presents the Morning Show for Radio Bristol

65. Eddie Scarlett, engineer on the site of the new William Budd Health Centre, Knowle West

66. Roy Bedford, Mark Wrigley, Tony Green and Mike Green, working on the new William Budd Health Centre at Knowle West Health Park

67. Julie Graham decorating angel whirls in the kitchen at Brimsham Green School, Yate

68. Emma Graham marking media studies work at John Cabot City Technology College

69. Martin Castledine, head verger at Bristol Cathedral, setting up for the 12.30 Communion Service

70. Steve Hassell, a blind piano tuner at Mickleburgh's in Stokes Croft

71. Behind the counter at Partco Ltd, Feeder Rd

72. Mrs Hazel Limb at work in the cloakrooms at Stockwood Green Primary School

73. Keith Bull, porter, emptying rubbish into the compactor outside Bristol Dental Hospital

74. A drayman from Butcombe Bitter delivering at the Wagon and Horses, Stapleton Rd

75. Evening Post seller outside the Hippodrome

76

77

78

79

76. Paul Popiel at work in the security and control room at Fry's factory
77. Bob Fawcett, the projectionist at Arnolfini
78. Tina Campbell on the phone at the Road Haulage Association, Cribbs Causeway
79. Alan Pitt and Jason Jones loading sand for cement at Florence Brown Special School, Knowle

80. Janet Robbins serving a customer at Jones The Bread, St George

81. Doug Steeds, postman, delivering a parcel in Knowle West

82. Simon Williams in his Chandos Rd Video Shop

83. Trevor Garlick repairing the wall at Nailsea Church

84. Philip Heaton and Matthew Limbear, upholsterers

85

86

87

88

85. Dr Huw Morgan catching up on paperwork at Corbett House Surgery, Barton Hill
86. Teresa Austin delivering sandwiches
87. Tim Rees on his mobile phone at work in Camera Corner, High Street, Bristol City centre
88. Meals on Wheels lady, Marion, delivering lunch in Lulsgate Rd, Bishopsworth

89

90

91

92

93

89. Richard Tovey of the Spar Shop in Chandos Rd

90. Darren Porch in the paintshop at the Bristol Old Vic

91. Abdia Hamed putting together a tumble dryer at the Creda factory in Yate

92. Rita Hudson making tea in the staffroom at Merrywood School

93. Julie King at work on alterations in K's Cleaners, Broad Street

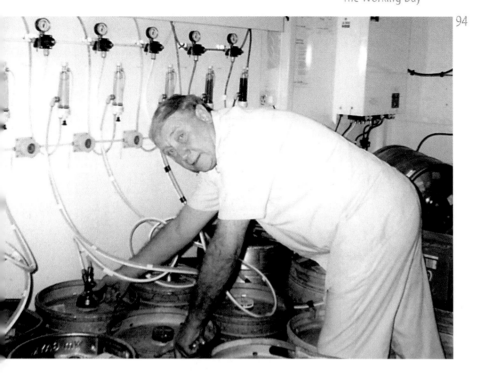

94

95

96

97

98

94. Les Smith in the cellar at the Albion, Portishead
95. Pat O'Driscoll putting up a sale sign on a house in Newbridge Rd, St Anne's Park
96. PCs Julie Williams and Marcus Claridge in Castle Park
97. Mr Stutt the butcher in Gloucester Rd
98. In the Bishopston hardware store on Gloucester Rd

99

100

102

101

57

99. Dean Watts sweeping up at J&D Tyres, Marsh Lane
100. John Singh sorting letters for the Post Office
101. Darren Wassell washing his hands at J&D Tyres, Marsh Lane
102. Leanne and Nick in the sergeant's office in Bridewell Police Station, central Bristol, at 2.15 am

103

104

105

106

103. Nick Thorne and Steve Forman outside the Shakespeare, Prince Street, after loading barrels of beer into the cellar
104. Mr Loxton by the sink in the wash room at the pathology lab, Weston-super-Mare Hospital
105. Collecting the bins in Court Rd, Bishopston
106. Eddie Coles busy in his garage in Winterbourne

5.
Health and Hospitals

The Childrens' Hospital, St. Michael's Hill. A new hospital is due to be completed by early next year on a new site in Maudlin St

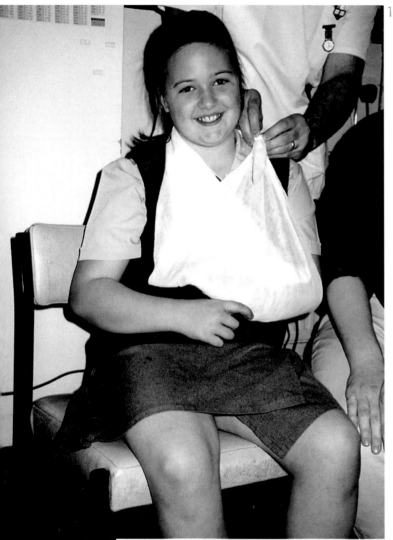

107

108

109

107. Miss Higgs having her arm sling adjusted in the
Outpatients Department of Bristol Childrens Hospital
108. Theatre nurse Wendy Russ in the neurosurgical ward
at Frenchay Hospital, about to set up for emergency surgery
on her night shift

109. Special baby Naomi Watkins, born on 27th April 1999,
after ten years of fertility treatments by her parents, being
held by nurse Margaret Hinder, at Clevedon Health Centre

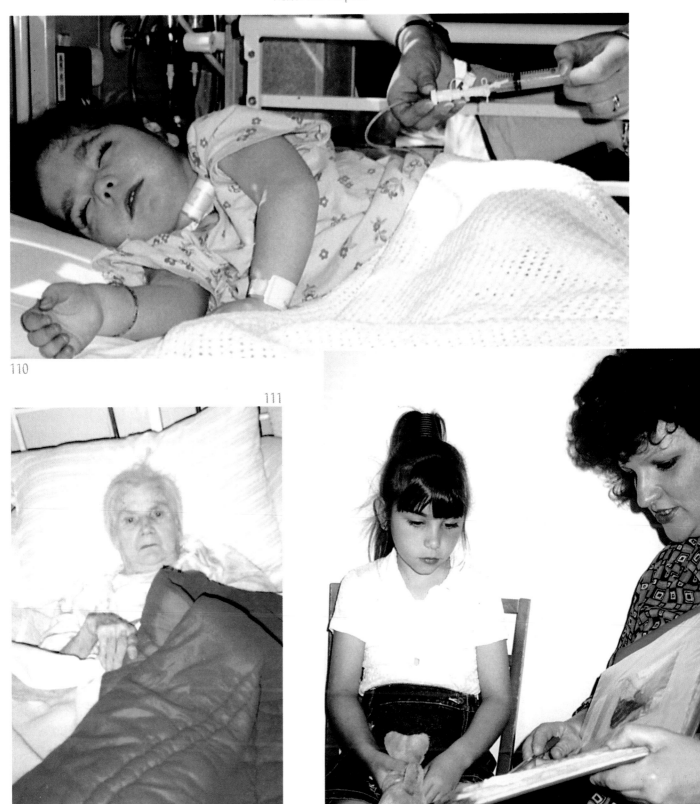

110. Three year old Naomi Fuller on Ward 36 of the Children's Hospital, recovering from a tracheotomy
111. Ninety eight year old Florence Herdman in her bed.
112. Pre-assessment with the play-leader at The Children's hospital

113

114

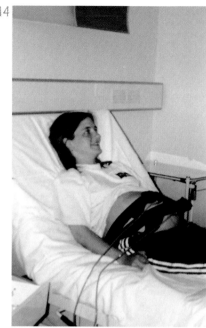

115

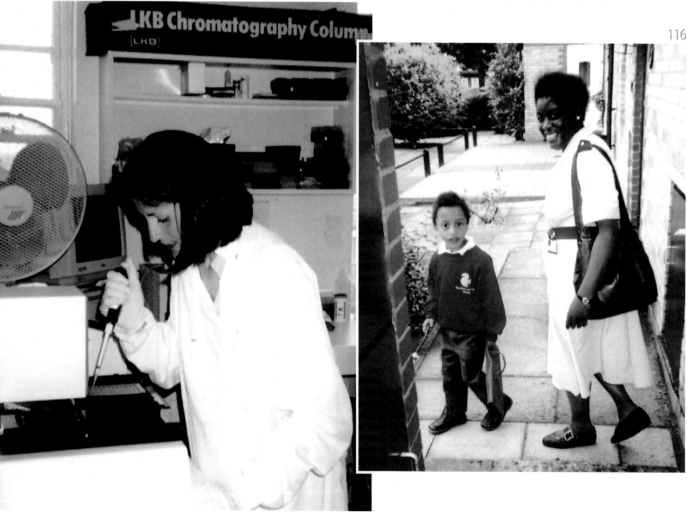

116

113. Edna Davis leaves the operating table at Bristol Eye Hospital, assisted by staff nurses Sally Ashton and Margaret Hooker
114. Zoe Hamet being monitored in the delivery suite at St. Michael's maternity hospital
115. Fay Stratton doing immunoglobulin analysis for the Children of the 90's Research Study at the Institute of Child Health laboratory, behind the Children's Hospital
116. Midwifery sister Beverley Willitts collecting her son Nicholas from school in Henbury

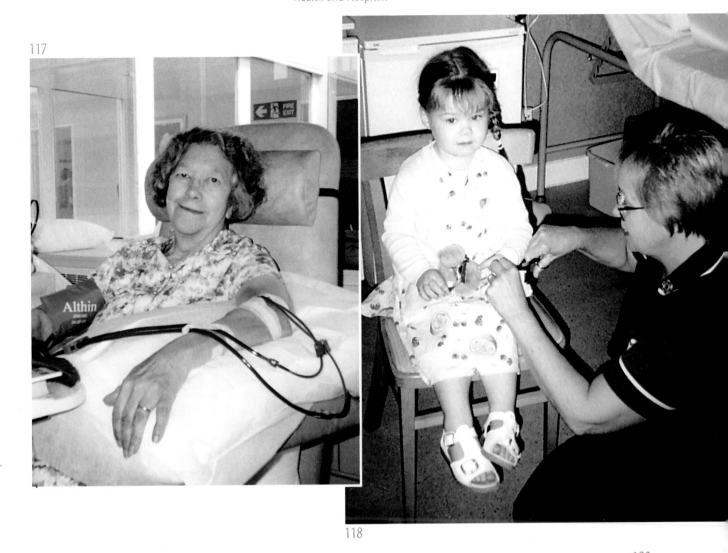

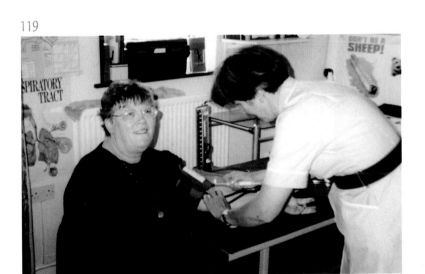

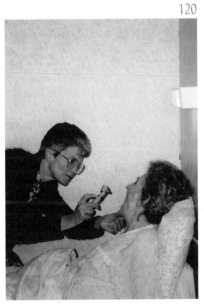

117. Grace Charles, a dialysis patient at the renal dialysis unit of the new Knowle West Health Park
118. Practice nurse Elizabeth Williams changing the bandage of young patient Alexa Jaworska
119. Maureen Dunsford having a blood sample taken by nurse Richardson at Corbett House surgery
120. Emily Blodwen Mitchell, a patient at Deerhurst Nursing Home, being examined by Dr. Judith Langfield

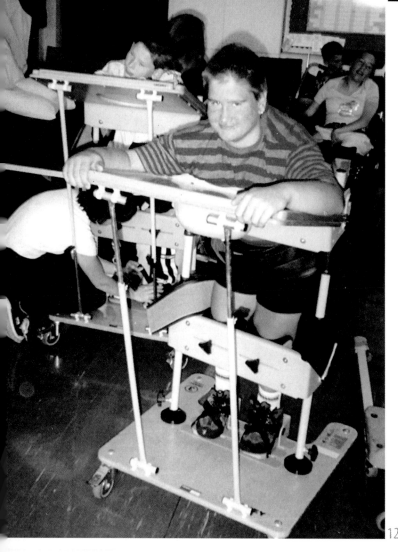

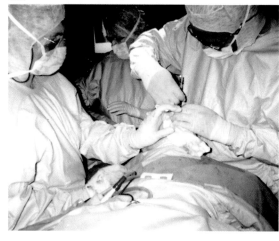

121. Jane, Kate and Simon in the main kitchen at St Monica home, Westbury-on-Trym
122. Zak Blacker in a standing frame at the Florence Brown Special School, Knowle
123. Knee surgeon David Johnson, aided by Chris Cruikshank, at the Chesterfield Nuffield Hospital

6.
Taking a Break

In a summery mood on
a bench in Broadmead

124. Two assistants from Sainsbury chatting outside Whiteladies Shopping Centre

125. Mr Godfrey studying Golf Monthly at home

126. Peter and Simon take five at Lawrence Weston Community Farm. The old minibus was destined to be recycled into a chicken coop the following week

127. Dave Pewsey having a cigarette break on the steps of the Avis Car Rental portacabin in Patchway

128

129

130

131

128. Tony Riga having a laugh on the golf course
129. A Bedminster teabreak
130. Lunch break at Ashton Park School - L-R are Jessica Ford, Gemma Creedy, and Thea Thompson-Cockcroft
131. Laura Cramer reading the Telegraph at work in the South West R.D.A.

132

133

134

132. Gos having a drink outside the Galleries
133. Alan Sainsbury filling up at Asda
134. Mr Ken Gore, Mr and Mrs Hodge, and Miss Beth Horlick playing croquet at St Monica Home, Westbury-on-Trym

135

136
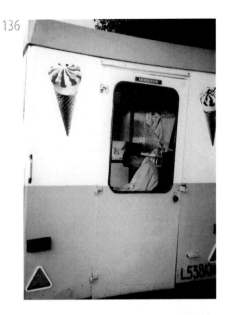

138

137

69

135. Sharing a pint and chips with the dog on the waterfront
136. Not much trade for this sleeping icecream salesman spotted in Castle Park
137. Coffee time at the Metro Cafe, Whiteladies Rd
138. John Vickery of Russell Grove, Westbury Park falling asleep in front of his television

139

140

141

139. Pete Hamson, Darren Ward and Gary Fry take a quick break from work at the new William Budd Health Centre, Knowle West

140. Sonya Rosen ordering her lunch at the Chesterfield Nuffield Hospital

141. A quiet moment in Stoke Bishop Village

7.
At School

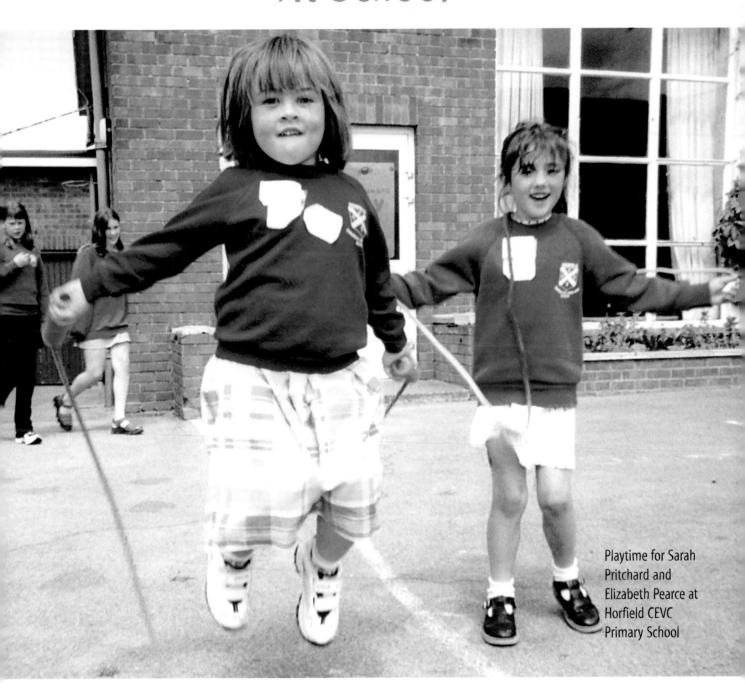

Playtime for Sarah
Pritchard and
Elizabeth Pearce at
Horfield CEVC
Primary School

142. Year 8 pupils at Brimsham Green School, Yate, showing off their pizzas - Mark Graham, Daniel Gardener, Catherine Elston, Lauren Thayer, Katie Lusby and Charlotte Wintle

143. Kim, Kira, Mignon, Daniel and Craig by the flowerbeds at Chester Park Infant School during lunch-time break

144. Peter Lunn in year 8 technology class, St Gregory's, Odd Down

145. Ms Howe's class at St Mary Redcliffe Primary

146. Children from Gay Elms School, Withywood, at Bishopsworth swimming pool

147. Steven Bates doing a wheelie by the bike sheds at Brimsham Green School, Yate, watched by James Murden and Nicola Pearson

148. Harvey, Ritchie and Ella, pupils at Chester Park Infant School, Lodge Causeway, are placing coins as part of the Kosovo Child Smile appeal

149. Mary Harrington and Marianna Fragapane in year 7 geography class, St Gregory's, Odd Down

150

151

152

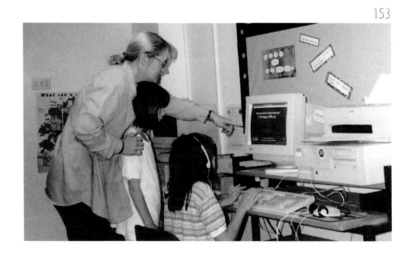

153

154

150. Music lesson at Brimsham Green School. Sarah Ormsby-Rymer on the horn, Sharon Lasek on the trombone and Shaun Wybrow on the cornet

151. Children at St Michael's C of E Primary School, Stoke Gifford, at playtime

152. Miss Joyce Harper's pre-primary ballet class, Henleaze

153. Mrs Debra Sanders with Louise Morgan and Sam Marshall on the computers at Parson Street Primary School

154. Ian Richards from Mangotsfield School photographing a horn for his artwork project

156

155

157

158

155. Kirsty McHugh revising in the sun at St Gregory's, Odd Down
156. Pupils of Cleeve House School, Wells Road, at their swimming lesson in the University pool, Clifton
157. End of year exam time at John Cabot City Technology College
158. Playtime at Nevers Lane junior school

159. Mrs Ann Fowles' violin class at Stockwood Green Primary School. The pupils (L to R) are Joan Baines, Louis Maddocks, Lauren Curtis and Natasha Jones

160. Mrs Bell, dinner lady, at playtime with children at Parson Street Primary School, Bedminster

161. Year 8's design and technology class at St Gregory's, Odd Down

162

163

164

165

162. Girls at Badminton School, Westbury-on-Trym, on the see saw
163. Mike Clark, Luke Hunter and Feiolim Eagles fooling about in their lunch hour at St Gregory's, Odd Down
164. Sophie Whiting and Shaun Callan busy at Southmead Day Nursery
165. Lee Reynolds and Matthew Leslie in the chemistry lab at John Cabot City Technology College

166

167

168

169

166. Off to camp - years 5 and 6 at Stockwood Green Primary School

167. The 2nd Winterbourne Brownie Pack having fun

168. Suki and Jodie's birthday party with school friends at Hawk's Gymn, Easton

169. Queuing for a drink at Horfield Primary School are (L to R) Jonathon Grose, Oliver Stokes, David Webber, Rosie-Beth Hickling, Fraser Haynes and Leah Brown

8.
Shopping

The magnificent glass and cast-iron roof of the Arcade shopping centre

169

170

171

172

173

174

169. Susan and Rachel Griffiths, and Alicia Emery beaming in the Bishopsworth Bakery

170. Hayley Griffin behind the counter at Bhogal's, the chemist shop in St Mark's Rd

171. Mrs Lucy Haskins, expectant mother, looks through the baby clothes in Mothercare

172. Fruit and vegetable display at Bonnie's in Bedminster

173. Joyce and Ken Kitteringham in Asda

174. Outside the Arcade, Kingswood, where shoppers often stop and rest

175

176

177

178

179

180

175. A worker from the Sickle Cell Thalassaemia Centre in Stapleton Rd, Easton

176. Richard Sweet making his selection at Sainsburys, Winterstoke Rd

177. Mona Treasure, Betty Carey and Leslie Peacey having a gossip outside Sainsburys on Whiteladies Rd

178. Trolley collecter Brian Jenkins at work outside Tesco, Bradley Stoke

179. The Metro Espresso on Whiteladies Rd

180. Traders on Gloucester Rd cover the pavements with their displays of goods

181. Mary working behind the sweet counter in Horfield Common Post Office
182. Rizwan in the Raja Stores, Easton
183. Oriental medicine practice in Westbury Park
184. Drink machines for thirsty fitness fans at Horfield Sports Centre
185. Judith Price working on the rottisserie in Asda

186

187

188

189

190

186. Shopworker Rebecca and her daughter outside Radford Mill Farm Shop in Picton Street, Montpelier
187. Mother and child in Broadmead
188. Andy Carter loading his van with bread and sandwiches for deliveries
189. Cocktail time at the Greenhouse, College Green
190. Doreen Moore and Albert Pearce taking the weight off their feet in East St., Bedminster

191

192

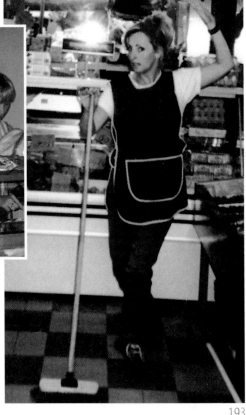

193

194

195

196

191. The Princes Pantry, a popular sandwich bar in Prime St

192. Charlie Howells and Angela Brown, pharmacists at Moss Pharmacy, Barton Hill

193. Olé! Carol O'Driscoll and her broom take a bow in the East St. Butchers, Bedminster

194. Buying icecream from Tony's van in Horfield

195. Dianne Edmonds, florist, in her shop at Barton Hill

196. Joshua Grotzke reading his comic to while away the time outside Tesco in Bradley Stoke

197

198

199

200

201

197. Mr Donald Colquhoun, formely worker of Northville Post Office, helping out behind the sweet counter in his son's post office

198. Owners and a friend in front of the Somalian take-away, Horn Of Africa, in Ashley Rd, St Pauls

199. The owner in front of Nirwan Fashions, St Mark's Rd, Easton

200. Maurice Hibbert's shop, St Mark's Rd, Easton

201. Sandra Demer behind the counter in the corner shop in Kingsdown

202. Alex's Fruit Market on Gloucester Rd
203. The owners outside New York Lick in Easton
204. Busy shoppers in the Arcade, Broadmead
205. Having coffee outside the Bristolian Cafe, Montpelier

9.
Our Pets

Doreen Rawlinson with her dog Tia in her garden at Meadow Vale, Speedwell

206

207

208

206. Ben Stockwell with his pet boxer, Peggy
207. Belinda Evans and Will Lee with their dogs
208. A family on the Downs sharing their icecream with their dog

209

210

211

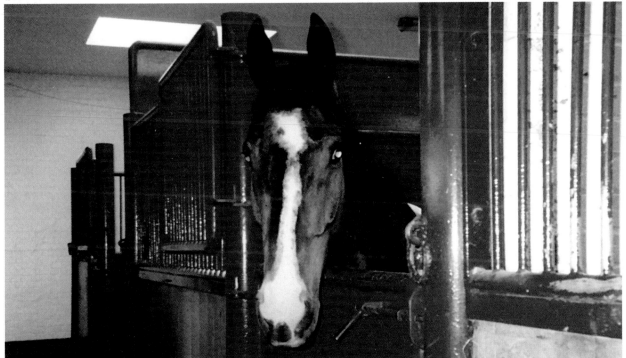

209. Big Issue seller with his Yorkshire terriers outside the Galleries
210. Hannah Kelly tickling her pet rabbit
211. Popular police horse Imperial in the police stables at Bower Ashton

212

213

212. Watering hole in the Gordano valley
213. Molly Perry playing in the back garden with her pet rabbit

10.
Getting Around

Mike Canning pushing
Francesca Senior who looks
sweet in a wheelbarrow made
for two

214

215

214. Circus trucks in the village field in Winterbourne
215. The car wash at the Elf Garage, on Coronation Rd

216

217

218

216. A Wessex dairies milk float making its way down Park St
217. The last journey: to Canford crematorium
218. Mrs Barnes boarding the free bus outside Sainsbury's Winterstoke Rd, assisted by bus driver Clive Dibbins

219

220

219. No takers for the Park and Ride bus at Long Ashton
220. Jeff Longdon maintaining the HGV training lorry at the HLTS Forklift Training Centre

11.
Body DIY

Keeping fit at the Greenway
Centre in Southmead

221

222

221. Warming up at Vicky's step class in Keynsham
222 Mrs Coles having a pedicure at Warr Court Elderly People's Home

224

223

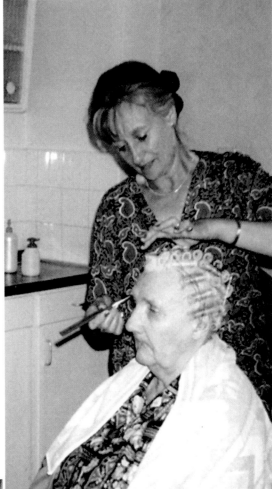

225

223. James Young in the gym at Viva Health Club

224. Ivy Moore having her hair done at Hollybrook Elderly People's Home

225. Joanna Martin, Vitali Cortesi and Carly Wish in the front row of the gymnastics class at Manor Park School

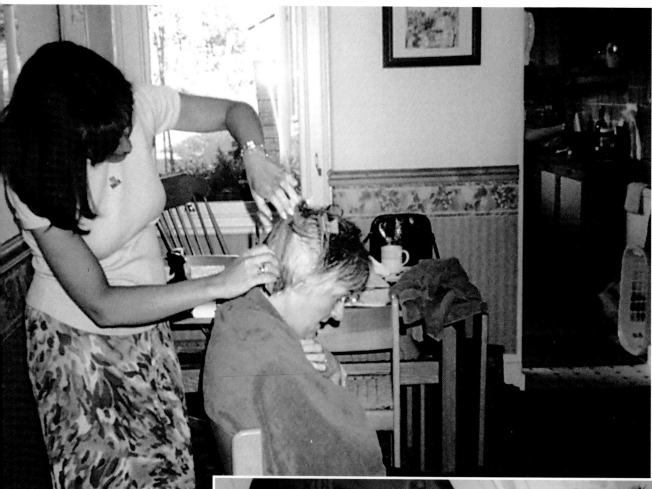

226

227

98

226. Mrs Joanne Ashcroft having her hair done by Amanda Hazelby in her dining room
227. Jennifer Smith putting mousse on her hair in Grampian Close, Oldham Common

12.
Out and About

Tom Humphries outside his home
in Braunton Rd, Bedminster in his
custom-built two-seater Triumph Herald
with a roadster body

228

229

230

228. Mr Fawley on the Downs, looking towards Avonmouth, and the Black Mountains of Wales beyond

229. Mrs Doreen Mallett at Bishopsworth Rd Post Office collecting her War Widow's pension

230. 7.45am on the 354 Nailsea to Bristol bus, going over the Cumberland Bridge, with the Suspension Bridge on the left

231

232

231. Cycling in St. George's Park
232. Simon Thomson buying a ticket from Patricia for a boat trip on the Bristol Packet

233. Eddy Coles at the Lloyds Bank cashpoint, Winterbourne
234. David and his dogs on his usual pitch on Whiteladies Rd
235. Katie Gargan throwing caution to the winds on the Torwood House garden slide

236

237

236. Three people from Newcastle pictured in front of a Stokes Croft mural on their way to the Glastonbury Festival
237. Piarra Singh at the parking ticket machine outside the maternity hospital on St. Michael's Hill

238

238. Catherine Hull walking to work with a South Bristol panorama in the background

239

239. An evening kite flyer on Durdham Down
240. Lunchtime sandwich eating in Brunswick Square

241

241. The shops at Inns Court in Knowle, known locally as Little Beirut due to the number of burnt-out and vandalised cars. The shops are soon to be demolished, and the shopkeepers will move across the road to new premises

242

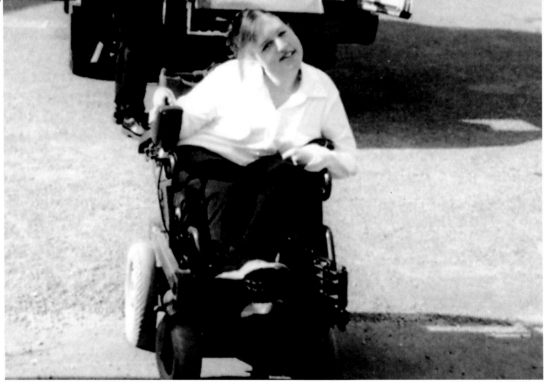

243

242. Carl Randall playing football by Portishead lake
243. Georgina Moore arriving at Brimsham Green School, Yate, by special taxi

244

245

244. D-Day veteran Ernest 'Sandy' Sandford (12th Para 6th Air Division) in North St., Bedminster
245. A Chelsea pensioner with his daughter and niece at the Watershed

246. Last light on Durdham Downs

13.
City Scapes

Pero's Bridge, better known as the horned
bridge, designed by Eilis O'Connell in 1998. It is
named after a black slave owned by the Piney
family of Bristol in the 18th Century

247

248

249

250

247. Relaxing on College Green, with Bristol Cathedral beyond

248. *Sentinel II* by Jim Paulsen (1993), one of 18 sculptures along the Bristol and Bath Railway Path and Sculpture Trail

249. The owner of Tony Caribbean Foods in front of the mural painted on the side of his shop

250. The *Gaius Sentius* drinking fountain by Gordon Young (1993) on the cycle path at Warmley

251

252

253

254

113

251. Monday is wash day in Avonmouth
252. A back view of the early Georgian houses on St. Michael's Hill, facing St. Michael on the Mount Without, taken from a crane on the new Children's Hospital site in Maudlin St
253. Balloon ascending at first light in Ashton Court
254. Prefabs at the corner of Risdale Rd and Langley Crescent, Ashton Vale

255. Looking up King St towards the Llandoger Trow
256. *Fish on its Nose* by Doug Cocker (1993) on the cycletrack at Fishponds
257. A stone arch leading to the award-winning garden of the Family Practice, Western College, Cotham
258. Looking over the old Colston almshouses, towards the Bristol university buildings

259

260

261

262

259. A fine Victorian wrought iron lamp outside the Corn Exchange

260. A dental nurse in front of a mural by Gloria Ojulari-Sule in Ashley Rd, St Pauls

261. Enjoying tea outside Baristas Tea House in Clare St

262. The tethered balloon on Castle Park. Installed in early summer 1999, it has now become a popular fixture of the landscape, giving unparalleled views of the city

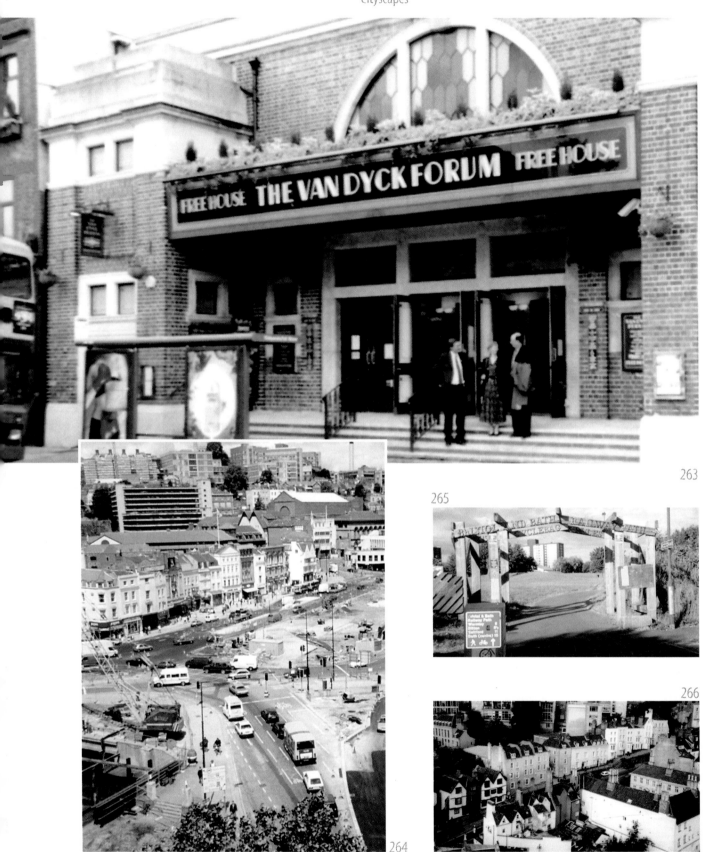

263

265

266

264

116

263. The Van Dyck forum, a former cinema and bingo hall in Fishponds
264. Developments in the City Centre, taken from the window of a 3rd floor office in Broad Quay House
265. The gateway to the 15 mile Bristol to Bath cycle path in Castle Park
266. The 17th and 18th century facades of St. Michael's Hill

267

268

269

270

267. Abbotswood shopping precinct, Yate
268. St. Michael on the Mount Without, with Park Row on the left
269. A tranquil break for an undisturbed Bristolian
270. The new Bristol and West building under construction at Temple Quay

271. Bruce and Pippa enjoying a romp in Blaise Woods

272. *The Fly* on the Emerald park roundabout, Kingswood

273. Behind the baricades at Bishopston community halls, protesting at moves by the Church of England to evict them to make way for a new community centre

14.
Children

A happy shopper with his
rabbit in Bristol city centre

274. Daniel Cutler swinging from the frame in his back garden
275. Suki and Jodie's party at Bristol Hawks gym in Easton
276. Happy dancers at the Bedminster Down Girls' Club

277

278

277. Tiva and Monique eating ice-cream on Stapleton Rd
278. Little Acorns aged four and five at Badminton School, Westbury-on-Trym

279

280

281

279. Pamela with Connor Moreton, born June 17 1999
280. James Partridge with his skateboard in Sandbach Rd, Brislington
281. Jon Notton looking into a cloudy Knowle sky

283

282

284

282. Pupils of the Florence Brown Special School in Knowle playing football before school begins
283. Charlie Warrington, aged eight, reading in bed before lights out in The Green, Stoke Gifford
284. Hayley and Charlotte Davis out for the count after lunch in Salcombe Rd, Knowle

285

286

287

285. Guides Marie and Carly Pritchard of Whitcroft Way, Kingswood

286. Walking home from school along Wordsworth Rd, Horfield

287. Donna and Faye Allen with friends Georgia Williams and Leanne Smeal, playing outside their house in St. George

288

289

290

125

288. Children playing on the swings in the park at Stoke Gifford

289. Joshua Grotzke and his friend Ben in the playshed

290. Robert waiting for his mum to finish shopping, in Chandos Rd

291. New-born Alfie Reeves being weighed by the midwife
292. Mending the vaccum cleaner in Bradley Stoke
293. Alexander Jones of Clyde Rd., Knowle, being given a bottle by his dad

294

295

296

294. Street games in Brislington
295. Maisie, Joel, Suki and Callum having a laugh on the bus
296. Annie White in mid-somersault

297

298

299

297. Twins Luke and Ella Harrison in Canford Park
298. Alan Swatton in mid-header
299. Natalya Hurley and Alexandra Ingram at their childminder's house

301

300

302

300. Ben Ward, Sandy Harvill and a friend exploring the playground train at Torwood House
301. Natalie Price sewing
302. Laura and Natalie falling off their skateboard

303

304

303. Hannah Kelly and her sister Alexandra trying on mum's new birthday bra at 23 Langton Rd, Brislington
304. Children in the youngest age group at Fromeside Gym Club

15.
Having Fun

Bradley Jenkins and
friends outside the
Waterfront Pub,
late evening

305

306

307

309

308

305. Bowling at Redland Green for the County Cup

306. Adam Thomkins flashing his tongue stud

307. Street games outside Bristol Hawks gym in Easton

308. The Bristol Water Festival viewed from the Arnolfini

309. Two lady vergers at Bristol Cathedral

310

312

313

311

314

310.   Andrew Oldroyd and Michelle Tedder, members of the
Tango West Dance Group, entertaining residents at
Alexandra Elderly People's Residential Home, Thornbury
311.   Tom Evans playing drums at the John Cabot City
Technical College

312.   Drama group at the City of Bristol College
313.   In the Foresters Arms, Gloucester Rd
314.   Early evening drinks at the Warwick, Kingswood

315. Mr Thomas filling out his Bristol Evening Post photography form at 17.41 precisely!
316. Bristol Old Vic Theatre School: Chris Harris directing students in *Mansfield Park*
317. Tulan Shah and Helen Webster of the Tango West Dance Group
318. Mike the bingo caller at the Riva
319. Mrs Robinson on bingo night at the Riva, Fishponds

320. Success at the fishing lake in Winterbourne
321. In a betting shop on Gloucester Rd
322. Roy Ball discussing his model railway with his mate Ian Whitlam
323. Janet Edmunds and Kate O'Leary, tutors at the City of Bristol College
324. Bill Cooper refining details on his model

325

326

327

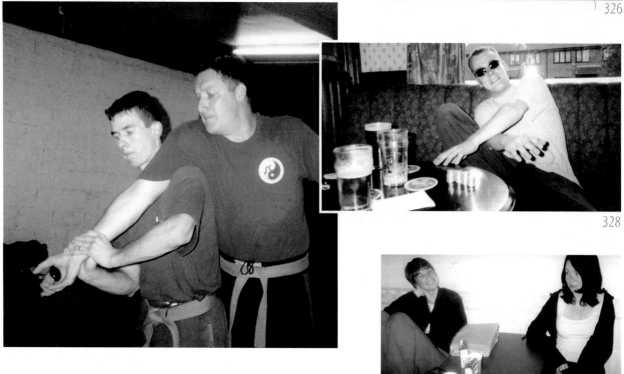

328

329

325. Cathy Batten and Kelly Clark having an evening drink at the Sedan Chair
326. Maurice Kirkby observing the moon through his telescope
327. Jim Newton and his son Jonathan practising jujitsu at Horfield Sports Centre
328. Phil with his winnings at the Warwick, Kingswood
329. Claire Dando and Jo Glossenbury, students on a child care course at Soundwell College, in the refectory

16.
End of the Day

Brunel's famous
Suspension Bridge,
lit at night

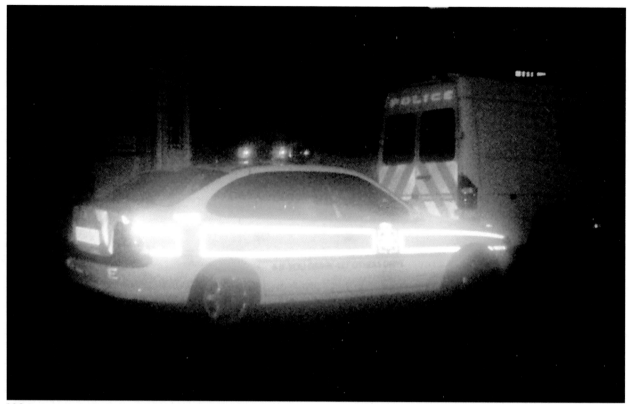

330

331

330. Outside Bridewell Police Station in central Bristol
331. Sunset from the roof garden on the Evening Post building, Temple Way

332

333

332. Wardour Rd, Bedminster, at dusk
333. Evelyn's fish and chip shop, Bedminster, in the early evening

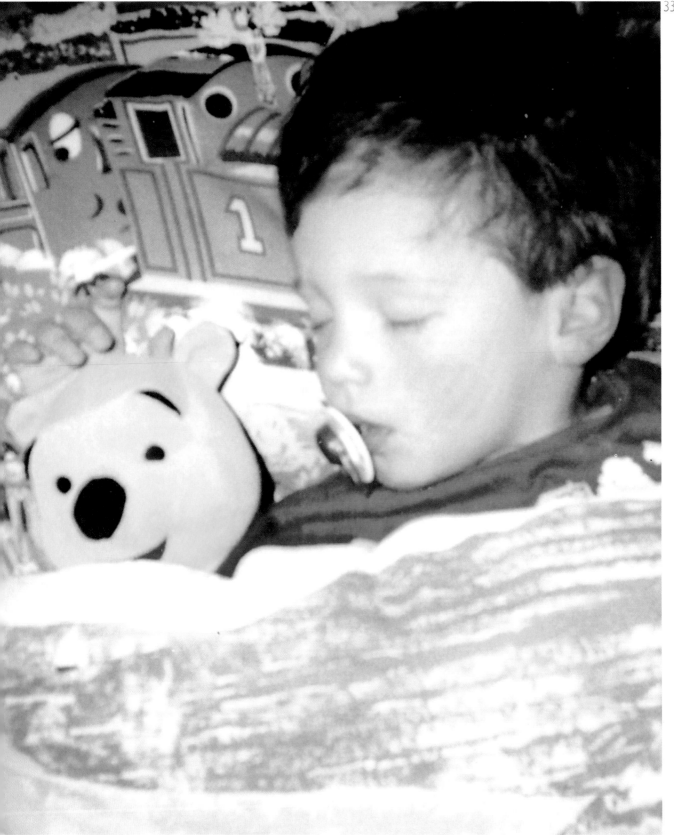

334. Callum Higgins and Winnie the Pooh at the end of the day

List of Contributors

Mrs Heather Allen, 24 Northcote Rd St. George
Shaun Allford, 25 Belluton Rd, Knowle, BS4
Mrs Sally Ashton, 19 Beverley Avenue, Downend, Bristol BS16 6SX
Ms Teresa Austin, 5 Coombe Lane, Stoke Bishop, Bristol BS9 2AB

Mrs Christina Baker, 248 Whiteway Rd St George BS5 7RS
Mrs S Baker, 44 Stackpool Rd, Southville, Bristol BS3 1NQ
Miss S.L. Barnes & Miss H.P. Barnes, 14 Ashgrove Road, Bedminster, Bristol BS3 3JW
Clare Barrington-Chappell, 1st Floor Flat, 6 Richmond Hill, Bristol BS8
Mr John S. Bickell, 10 Longleat Close Henleaze BS9 4LP
Rosemary Blackmore, 7 Milton Hill, Weston-s-Mare BS22 9RA
Ray Brooking, 19 Peal St. Bedminster BS3 3OZ
Mrs Maureen Brown, 38 Broadfield Avenue, Kingswood, Bristol, BS15 1HY
Lisa Bryant, 35 Quarry Barton Hambrook BS16 1SG
Maggie Buist, Marketing Co-ordinator, The Chesterfield Nuffield Hospital
Mr Jason Burgess, 28 Parkwall Rd Longwell Green BS30 8HL
Claudia Burton, 65 Filton Grove Horfield BS7 0AW

Jane Campbell, Lawrence Weston Community Farm, Saltmarsh Drive, Bristol BS11 0ND
Martin Castledine, Head Verger Bristol Cathedral
Catherine Chadd, 30 Apseleys Mead, Bradley Stoke, Bristol BS32 0BG
Graham Clark, 5 Abbots Close, Windways Whitchurch BS14 0ND
Miss Kelly Clark, 89a Saltmarsh Drive, Lawrence Weston, Bristol, BS11 0NL
Paul Clark, 4 Greendale Rd Bedminster BS3 5EW
Sharon Clark, Arts Press Officer, Bristol Old Vic
Frances Cole Hollybrook Elderly People's Home 499 Hareclive Rd Bristol BS13 0JP
Mrs Jenny Coles and Mr E Coles, 37 Watleys End Rd Winterbourne BS36 1PH
Sophie Collin, 84 Bedminster Rd Bedminster
Mr M and Mre E.E. Coggins, 12 Tregarth Rd Ashton Vale BS3 2QS
Michael John Comley, 41 Elm Road, Bristol, BS15 9ST, Kingswood
Mrs Patt Cooper, 18 Park Road, Southville, Bristol, BS3 1PU
Tracy Comer c/o Evening Post
Barbara Cornish, 4 Sandy Lodge Yate
Hannah Cottrell, 402 St John's lane, Bedminster, Bristol BS3 5BA

Chris Darch, 26 Maple Walk, Keynsham BS31 2SB
Mrs J. Davis, 14 Harrington Ave, Stockwood, Bristol
Mrs Maria Jane Davis, 34 Sallcombe Rd, Knowle BS4 1AO
Caroline Davy, 2 Chew Cotts, Dapps Hill Keynsham BS31 1EU
Tim Davy, Bristol Evening Post
Miss Tracey Devine, 42 Goldcrest Rd Chipping Sodbury
Linda Donovan, 8 Greenwood Rd, Knowle Park, BS4 2SX

James Ellis, 28 Effingham Rd, St Andrews, Bristol, BS6 5JB
Elaine Ennis, 19 Lorain Walk Henbury BS10 7AS

Kirstie Ford, 51 Leaholme Gardens, Whitchurch, Bristol
Steve Foulkes, 269 Wick Rd Brislington BS4 4HR

Philip Gannaway, 1 Meadow Vale, Speedwell Bristol BS35 7RG
D. Godfrey, 3 Maynard Close Bristol BS13 0AR
Katharin Goodland, 14 Rodney Rd Backwell Somerset BS48 3HR
Royston Green, 27 Elton Rd, Kingswood, Bristol BS15 1NQ
Philip Grey, 44 Sandown Road, Brislington, Bristol BS4 3PN
Mrs Alison Grotzke, 30 Ormonds Close, Bradley Stoke, BS32 0DX
Darren Guy, 253 Wordsworth Rd Horfield BS7 0EE

Jenny Hall, 45 Archer Walk Stockwood BS14 8LF
Robert Hambley, 92 Palmers Leaze, Bradley Stoke
M.A. Hancock, 320 Bishopsworth Rd, Bristol BS13 7LJ
Francis Harford, 82 Colston Rd, Easton, Bristol BS5 6AD
H. Harris, 17 Highmead Gardens, Withywood Bristol BS13 8NP
Corin Harrison, 6 Waters Lane, Westbury-on-Trym
Sarah Heaton, c/o Torwood House Nursery School
J. Henderson, 215 Soundwell Rd Kingswood BS15 1PT
Ellie Higgins, 6 Redfield Rd Patchway BS34 6PH 0
June Rowena Hillier, 29 Dunkfield Avenue, Filton BS37 7RH
Mrs L. Hole, 10 Park Ave, Bedminster, Bristol
Pat Holmyard, Wood Lodge, Valley Rd, Leigh Woods, Bristol BS8 3PZ
David Hounsome, 37 Crowthern Rd Horfield Bristol
Andrew Hudd, 29 Signall Rd Staple Hill Bristol BS16 5PF
Dave and Lin Hughes, 102 Filton Ave Horfield
Catherine Hull, 22 Downend Rd Horfield BS7 9PF
Mrs W.J. Humphries, 9 Merrimans Road, Bristol
Jacqueline Hurley, 44 Beechcroft Pinkhams Twist Whitchurch BS14 0SF

Patricia Irwin c/o Pembroke Guest House, 83 Coronation Rd Bristol BS3 1AT

Pamela Jehoris, 14 Berkshire Rd, Bishopston
Vicky Jones, 30 Clyde Rd, Knowle, Bristol

Phillip and Wendy Kelly, 23 Langton Rd, Brislington, Bristol BS4 4EP
Ross Kilpatrick, 6 Logan Rd, Bristol
Maurice & Rina Kirby, 3 West Town Ave, Brislington, Bristol BS4 5DH

Dr. Judith Langfield, 11 Haynes Lane Staple Hill BS16 5JE
Isobel Larcombe, 19 Church Rd, Hanham, Bristol
Chris Lillington, 23 Grange Rd, Bishopsworth, Bristol BS13 8LE
John E. Llewellyn-Jones, 43 Watermore Close, Frampton Cotterell, Bristol BS36 2NQ
Mrs Lynne Lovell, 40 Church Lane Backwell BS48 3PQ
John Loxton, 35 Paddock Park Worle BS22 6BW

Shirley Macleod, 11 Cotham Side Bristol BS6 5TP
Allison Lucieme McCallum, 72 Oaktree Cres. Bradley Stoke North BS32 9AD
Phil Madden/ Jane Madden
Angela Maggs, 10 Court Rd, horfield, Bristol, BS7 0BT
Mrs Doreen Mallett, 7 Lulsgate Rd, Bristol BS13 7A
Richard Mallett, 25 Coombe Bridge Ave Stoke Bishop BS9 2LT
Jean Maloney, 60 Calcott Rd Knowle BS4 2HE
Mrs Rose Manning, 19 Wexford Road, Knowle West, Bristol BS4 1PU

Michael Manson, 92 Sefton Park Rd, Bristol, BS7 9AL
Mrs Susan Marshall, 8 Warren Lane, Long Ashton
Miss Suzanne Marshall, 13c Court Rd, Kingswood, Bristol
Mary Moller, 2 Leighview Rd Portishead BS20 7ED
Julie Morris,117 Stackpool Rd, Southville, BS3 1NY
Angela Moore, 22 Morley Rd, Staple Hill, Bristol
Stephen Morris, Garden Flat, 1 Elmgrove Road, Redland, Bristol BS6 6AH
Steve Moss, 9 Alexandra Rd, Uplands Bristol BS13 7DF
L.G. Murray, 70 Hawkridge Drive, Bristol

Johnnie and Jilly Nickolls, 49 Wick Crescent, Brislington, BS4 4HG
Eileen Noble, 19 Wesley Lane Warmley BS30 8BN

Kevin O'Hagan, 26 Alpine Road, Easton, Bristol, BS5 6BD
Debbie Oppery, 109 Willis Road, Kingswood, Bristol
R. Osborne, 176 Broomhill Rd, Bristol, BS4 4TD

Linda Page, 45 Sylvan Rd Sea Mills
Miss Alex Parker, 25 St Bedes Rd, Kingswood, BS15 1QA
Dawn Parsons, 67 Rookery Rd Knowle Bristol BS4 2DX
Karen Partridge, 5 Sandbach Rd, Brislington, Bristol
Mrs D.G. Payne, 74 Silbury Rd Bristol
Mrs Lynda Payne, Southmead Day Nursery, Doncaster Rd, Southmead, BS10 5PW
John and Margaret Peacock, 30 Chandos Rd, 34 Farington Rd Westbury-on-Trym
Roy Pepworh, 8 Southfield Court Westbury-on-Trym
Patrick Clive Perry, 16 Grampian Close Oldland Common BS30 8QA
Martin R.A. Pick, 19 Holywell Close, St Annes Park Bristol
Ms J Price, 16 Lapwing Gardens, Frenchay, Bristol BS16 1UB
Rachel Price, 4 Bell Close Bishop Manor Rd Bristol BS10 5DF
Marie Pritchard, 34a Whitecroft Way, Kingswood, Bristol, BS15 9YN
Elizabeth Prowse, 35 Risdale Rd Bristol BS3 2RA

Miss Angela Reynolds, 88a Silver Street, Nailsea
Mr P.J. Richards, 32 Lanercost Rd Southmead Bristol BS10 6HN
J. Richards, 37 Berkeley Rd, Bishopston, Bristol, BS7
Christine Rose, 11a Druid Rd Stoke Bishop BS9 1LJ
Mrs Melanie Rowbottom, 33 Brockley Close Little Stoke Bristol BS34 6HA

Janette Sainsbury, 9 Fitchett Walk, Henbury BS10 7LQ
Mrs D. Sanders, 63 Brighton Cres Bedminster BS3 3PP
Mr A. G. Shelper, 4 Courville Close Alveston BS35 3RR
Francesca Senior, 5 Kingscourt Close, Whitchurch BS14 9QP
Matthew Shelley, Features Dept Evening Post
Dr W. Sinton, Flat 2, Westfield house, Cote Lane, Bristol BS9 3UL
Carol Sleight, 65 Pooles Wharf Court BS8 4PD
T.V. Slocombe, 10 Harrington Drive Keynsham BS31 1YA
Dorothy Smith, 85 Silbury Rd Bristol BS3 2QE
Mr M.P. Smith 5 Grampian Close, Oldham Common Bristol BS30 8QA
Sarah Smith, 7 Ham Green Hill, Ham Green
Veronica Smith, 39 St Markís Rd Bristol BS5 0LN
Isabel Speed, 16 Alexandra Rd Bristol BS8 2DD
Patricia Stanley, 20 Dubbers Lane Brsitl BS5 7EL
Margaret Mary Staynings, 8 The Coppice, Bradley Stoke, Bristol BS32 8DY
Pam Stockwell, 111 New Road, Stoke Gifford, BS34 8TFWendy Stone, 31 Berenda Drive, Longwell Green BS30 9YX
Michele Stokes, 45 Wellington Walk Bristol
Rob Stokes, Assistant Editor Evening Post
Mrs Frances Stutt, 21 Wardour Rd, Knowle, Bristol, BS4 1SE

Ms Rosemary Sygrave, Flat 26 The Beeches, Salisbury Rd, St Annes Park, BS4 4ES
Mark Taylor, Features Dept Bristol Evening Post
Michele Tedder, 20 Manxse Rd, Knowle Bristol BS4 2JG
I. Thomas, 65 Dominion Road, Fishponds, Bristol
Mrs B. M Thompson, 68 Ventnor Rd, St. George BS5 7SH
Mrs C.J. Thompson, 17 Benville Ave, Coombe Dingle, Bristol
Imogen Thynne, 12 Milford St Bristol
Basil Townsend, 7 Miles Rd Bristol BS8 2JN
Michael Trim, 14 Badgers Walk, Brislington, Bristol BS4 4LG
Kath Tudor & Janet Edmeades c/o City of Bristol College
Mair Turner, 66 Wolfridge Ride Bristol
Miss Susan Tyte, Chester park Infants School, Lodge Causeway, Fishponds, Bristol

Margaret Venn, 50 Court Rd, Kingswood, Bristol BS15 9QG
Mrs Fran Vickery, 48 Russell Grove, Bristol BS6 7UF
Paula Vicary, 56 Campion Drive Bradley Stoke BS32 0BH

Mr J.C. Young, 78 Coronation Rd, Bristol, BS3 1AT
James Young, 35 Eastfield Rd Westbury-on-Trym BS9 4AE

Bernadette Walker, 19 Oldbury Court Rd Fishponds
Anthony Walsh, 31 Logan Rd, Bishopston, Bristol BS7 8DS
Maureen Warner, 62 Gordan Avenue, Whitehall, Bristol BS5 7DS
Mr & Mrs G & M Warner, 62 Gordon Ave, Whitehall, Bristol BS5 7DS
Penny Warner c/o Stockwood Green Primary School, Stockwood Lane Bristol BS14 8S
Charlotte Warren, 15 Gaynor Road, Filton BS7 0SP
Jennie Warrington, Wayside 9 The Green Stoke Gifford
Johanne Watts, 108 Hareclive Rd, Hartcliffe, BS13 9JR
Jackie Webber, 32 Barrowhill Road, Shirehampton, Bristol
Mrs J. Whatley, 80 Coleford Rd, Southmead, Bristol
Jaqui Wilcox, 65 Ravenhill Rd, Lower Knowle
Mr R Williams, 24 Crossfield Rd, Staple Hill, Bristol BS16 4SJ
Beverley Willitts, 1A Didsbury Close Henbury BS10 7AB
Elisabeth Winkler, 8 Monk Road, Bristol BS7 8LE
Jessica Winkler (no address supplied)
Caroline Worgan, 4 Newcheltenham Rd Kingswood BS15 1TH10
Caroline Wright, 46 Elm Park Filton BS34 7PP
Jill Wring, Charnwood House, Frog lane, Filton Bristol